# W

HYPOMNEMATA

V&R

# HYPOMNEMATA

## UNTERSUCHUNGEN ZUR ANTIKE
## UND ZU IHREM NACHLEBEN

Herausgegeben von
Albrecht Dihle/Hartmut Erbse/Christian Habicht
Hugh Lloyd-Jones/Günther Patzig/Bruno Snell

HEFT 87

VANDENHOECK & RUPRECHT IN GÖTTINGEN

MALCOLM HEATH

# Political Comedy
# in Aristophanes

VANDENHOECK & RUPRECHT IN GÖTTINGEN

Published with assistance from the Jowett Trust
and other benefactors.

*CIP-Kurztitelaufnahme der Deutschen Bibliothek*

*Heath, Malcolm:*
Political comedy in Aristophanes / Malcolm Heath. –
Göttingen: Vandenhoeck u. Ruprecht, 1987
(Hypomnemata; H. 87)
ISBN 3-525-25186-6
NE: GT

© Vandenhoeck & Ruprecht in Göttingen 1987 –
Printed in Germany.
Ohne ausdrückliche Genehmigung des Verlages ist es nicht gestattet,
das Buch oder Teile daraus auf foto- oder akustomechanischem
Wege zu vervielfältigen.
Satz: Dörlemann-Satz GmbH & Co. KG, Lemförde.
Druck: Hubert & Co., Göttingen

# Contents

# 1. Introduction

'This is a threadbare subject': so in 1938 Gomme introduced his influential paper on Aristophanes and politics, and the subject has been exposed to a good deal of wear and tear since he wrote those words.[1] A sense of tedium could be forgiven; but tempted though we may feel simply to abandon the whole issue and to seek new questions to discuss, the problem of political intent in Aristophanic comedy remains obstinately difficult to evade. Gomme, indeed, although he thought that some relatively easy deductions could be made about Aristophanes' political outlook,[2] argued at rather greater length that such deductions were of purely biographical interest, contributing nothing to our appreciation of the plays as plays.[3] But, quite apart from the perfectly valid objection that we need also to appreciate the plays as historical evidence, the antithesis on which Gomme rests his case between 'politician' and 'dramatist' is highly questionable. The notion of the politically motivated dramatist is a coherent one that should not be dismissed *a priori*, while the generalisation that 'for a dramatist there is no right or wrong side (whatever his private opinions may be)'[4] seems easily refuted by counterexample. One might still feel (as I do not) that political commitment necessarily impairs artistic or literary value;[5] but one is not then entitled to conclude that Aristophanes' work was not in fact so flawed until one has shown on independent grounds that it was not in fact so committed.

More recent trends in criticism might encourage the hope that the issue could be sidestepped if we were to treat the plays' political themes as part of the purely literary structure of each text, a structure that could in principle be grasped in abstraction from the text's intended bearing on extratheatrical political practice. This approach would be similar in its effect to Gomme's, though dressed up in a newer

---

[1] A. W. Gomme, 'Aristophanes and politics', *CR* 52 (1938) 97–109 (= *More Essays in Greek History and Literature* [Oxford 1962] 70–91).

[2] Gomme (n.1) 107–8.

[3] Gomme (n.1) 103–7.

[4] Gomme (n.1) 99.

[5] Cf. Gomme's revealing remark on *Knights*: 'I prefer to believe that ... his dramatic genius got the better of him; and that in fact he does not attack, but gives a picture of contemporary Athenian politics' ([n.1] 106 n.1).

theoretical language; yet here, too, we must insist that it is, in point of theory, flawed. A text is not simply a structure of words, sentences and themes; it is a teleological system – that is, it is words, sentences and themes organised with a view to some end: specifically, with a view to a communicative end of some kind. That is to say that a text characteristically envisages and invites some particular kind of reception; there is some (imprecisely defined) range of responses and effects which it is designed to elicit. Consequently, the structure of a text cannot be grasped correctly without reference to its communicative end (that is, its meaning). To understand Aristophanes' plays, therefore, we must ask about the reception with a view to which they were composed; and this will inevitably raise in turn the question of political intent.

But this question, though inescapable, is extremely difficult to answer – and is so for readily intelligible reasons. It is not simply that we lack the intimate knowledge of the contemporary world which Aristophanes presupposed of his audience, so that many allusions pass us by or baffle us. Even where we can detect and explain an allusion, its tone or point may elude us. Irony, fantasy and playful distortion are parts of the comic dramatist's repertoire, and they may present an almost insuperable interpretative barrier to 'outsiders', to those not antecedently familiar with the moods and intentions conventionally appropriate in a given comic genre. It would be an exaggeration to say that what seems to us *prima facie* plausible is probably for that very reason wrong; but it would be perfectly correct to insist that its seeming *prima facie* plausible to uninitiates like ourselves affords exceptionally weak grounds for supposing that it is probably right.

Ideally, therefore, one would wish to find some kind of external control, evidence independent of our reading of the plays that would help us to calibrate our estimation of their tone or mood. Evidence about the poet, for example, might usefully restrict the range of intentions which could plausibly be ascribed to him; evidence about his audience might help us to reconstruct the expectations and preferences with which he had to reckon, and so indicate the kinds of response and effect which he might have intended to achieve; evidence about the context in which a play was composed and received, and the consequent constraints on both poet and audience, might also help us to determine their respective intentions and receptive dispositions. That evidence of this kind is, by and large, not forthcoming will be painfully obvious; but we do have some evidence of the kind, and it is with this that we must begin our enquiry.

## 2. *Clouds*

I propose to begin by discussing *Clouds*. This is not itself a political play, but de Ste Croix refers to it in concluding his account of Aristophanes' political outlook.[6] Following Dover he finds in the play 'an invitation to violence, or oppressive legislation' against Socrates and other sophists, and in this he perceives an analogy for, and so a defence of, the intent to influence political opinion which he ascribes to the poet.[7] I shall argue, however, that in this case we do possess external evidence concerning Aristophanes himself which casts serious doubt on the interpretation proposed; and if we allow that evidence its proper weight, *Clouds* in fact supports by analogy a rather different approach to politics in Aristophanes.

The main witness here is Plato, and there are two crucial texts (passages such as *Phaedo* 70b10–c2 add nothing either way). First, *Apology*. In *Ap.* 18–19 Socrates distinguishes between his immediate and his more remote (and more formidable) accusers: between Anytus and his associates on the one hand, and on the other those who had for many years been building up a false and hostile public image for Socrates, and thus encouraging prejudice against him. It is suggested that a comic poet was one of the latter group (18d1–2); the description of Socrates' prejudicial public image is clearly modelled on *Clouds* (18b6–c1, 19b4–c1); and Aristophanes is eventually named as its source (19c2–4). Does this suggest hostility towards Socrates on Aristophanes' part, such as Dover and de Ste Croix envisage? It could be argued, on the contrary, that Plato implicitly distinguishes the comic poet of 18d1–2 from those of Socrates' remote accusers maliciously inclined (18d2–3 ὅσοι δὲ φθόνῳ καὶ διαβολῇ χρώμενοι ὑμᾶς ἀνέπειθον). But one must also ask *why* Plato chose to refer so insistently to comedy at this point. One possibility is that the treatment of Socrates in comedy did, in Plato's judgement, have the effect on public opinion that he describes. Were that so, it would be comprehensible whether or not *Clouds* and similar plays were written with that end in view, so that *Apology* does not, even on this interpretation, count in favour of hostile intent. But it is also possible that, by insinuating that the charges against Socrates at his trial were based on a lot of nonsense out of comedy (19b1–2 ἢ δὴ καὶ πιστεύων Μέλητός με ἐγράψατο τὴν

---

[6] G. E. M. de Ste Croix, *The Origins of the Peloponnesian War* (London 1972) 355–76 (= Appendix 29, 'The political outlook of Aristophanes').

[7] De Ste Croix (n.6) 371, quoting K. J. Dover (ed.), *Aristophanes: Clouds* (Oxford 1968) lvi.

γραφὴν ταύτην), Plato's intention was to discredit the prosecution's case; compare the ironical thrust in 19c7: 'I mean no disrespect for such knowledge, if anyone is really versed in it – I do not want any more lawsuits brought against me by Meletus.'[8] If that were Plato's intention, it would mean that he felt able to count on a general acceptance that comic portrayals were untrue and should not influence opinion outside the theatre (I shall argue in this paper that this would in fact have been generally recognised); this in turn would count against the ascription to Aristophanes of hostile intent against his victims.

*Apology* proves inconclusive, therefore; *Symposium* is more helpful. In this dialogue we find Aristophanes associating on apparently friendly terms with Socrates and other members of the Socratic circle, such as Agathon and Alcibiades – the very people he habitually satirises in his plays as progressive intellectuals.[9] The mere co-presence of Socrates and Aristophanes at Agathon's party is indecisive; it could have been a tactless error on Agathon's part – although we should note that the host was himself not exempt from Aristophanes' mockery;[10] that his two guests do not appear to be on unfriendly terms (note the amicable banter in 177e1–2); and that Alcibiades is able to quote *Clouds* without apology in an encomium of its victim (221b1–4). Also indecisive is the fact that Aristophanes is engaged in philosophical discussion with Socrates and Agathon at the very end of the dialogue (223c4–d6); not all of Socrates' partners in discussion were willing and sympathetic. But such evasions seem rather pointless when we find Alcibiades including Aristophanes by name in his enumeration of those present who have 'shared in the passion for philosophy' (218a7–b4 πάντες γὰρ κεκοινωνήκατε τῆς φιλοσόφου μανίας τε καὶ βακχείας). Alcibiades is, it is true, drunk; but though this relaxes his inhibitions, it does not seem to impair his reliability as a witness: his encomium of Socrates is meant, after all, to be believed.

Plato goes to some lengths to secure verisimilitude in *Symposium*, and it seems unlikely that he has abandoned this quest for the verisimilar in the single case of Aristophanes. We must assume, therefore,

---

[8] H. Tredennick (tr.), *The Last Days of Socrates* (Harmondsworth 1954) 21.

[9] There is a sensible discussion by G. Daux, *REG* 55 (1942) 237–58; see also Dover, *JHS* 86 (1966) 41–50.

[10] In addition to *Thesm.*, see frr. 169=178, 326=341. (Comic fragments are cited according to Kock's enumeration, with references to Kassel-Austin added where available, i.e. for Aristophanes [vol. III/2], for Callias and Cratinus [vol. IV], and for Eupolis [vol. V].)

that the inclusion of Aristophanes as an active member of the Socratic circle accords with known facts, although his account of the particular occasion is doubtless fictitious.[11] There is some corroborative evidence for this view in contemporary comedy. Cratinus could refer to a hypothetical member of the audience (perhaps in a context similar to *Peace* 43-8) as a 'clever, hypersubtle connoisseur of little conceits, a Euripidaristophanizer': κομψός τις . . . θεατής, ὑπολεπτολόγος, γνωμιδιώκτης, εὐριπιδαριστοφανίζων (fr. 307=342). The association of Euripides and Socrates is a commonplace in comedy,[12] and Cratinus characterises his 'euripidaristophanist' in language equally applicable to Socrates himself (cf. *Clouds* 319-21). Thus Cratinus' fragment is a jibe implying that Aristophanes is himself another of those tiresome over-subtle intellectuals, like Euripides and their common mentor Socrates. At least one contemporary's perception of him, therefore, was consonant with the implications of *Symposium*.[13]

Interesting consequences follow. If the poet of *Clouds* was indeed on amicable terms with Socrates and sympathetic to the intellectual interests of his circle, then we cannot safely infer, here or elsewhere, from gross distortions in a comic portrayal to the poet's ignorance of or indifference to the truth about the individual portrayed, nor from extreme abuse and even violence on the comic stage to the poet's hostility towards or disapproval of the victim outside the theatre. It must be acknowledged that the external evidence on which this conclusion is based is neither as full nor as secure as one would like; but there is *no* worthwhile counterevidence external to the play at all, so that this conclusion can be set aside only by those who place more

---

[11] Dover expresses doubts about the 'biographical relevance' of *Symp.*: 'my own view is that by presenting the story of Agathon's party as a story told by Apollodorus at second hand many years after the event Plato is clearly warning that he wants us to judge it by its quality and utility (as we would judge a myth), not by its relation to fact' ([n.7] xx n.3). But (i) Plato has obscured this point by making Apollodorus insist that he has verified the details with Socrates himself (173b1-6); and (ii) we are entitled to ask how presenting Aristophanes as an active member of the Socratic circle (as we have seen, it is not adequate to say simply that Plato 'represents him as a guest at Agathon's house') enhances the 'quality and utility' of the dialogue.

[12] Aristophanes fr. 376=392 (from the first *Clouds*), Telecleides frr. 39, 40, Callias fr. 12=15; cf. D.L.2.18.

[13] This seems not to have been the only attempt to associate Aristophanes with Euripides; in fr. 471=488 we find him apparently defending himself against such a charge – ironically, by means of a subtle *distinguo*. (For other jokes against Aristophanes used more than once by his rivals, see the scholia to *Ap.* 19c.)

confidence in their ability to assess the play's tone without external
guidance than seems, on grounds of general principle, to be war-
ranted.


## 3. Knights

We have no evidence external to the plays to tell us about Aristophanes' political activities and sympathies; the kind of control which we
applied to *Clouds* is therefore not available when we turn to the
political plays proper. Nevertheless, we do have even here relevant
kinds of external data which may help us to make some tentative
inferences.

First of all, we can correlate the reception enjoyed by Aristophanes'
plays inside the theatre with the political behaviour of his audiences
outside. The most striking datum here is provided by *Knights*. Aristophanes won first prize with this play, devoted to virulent abuse of
Cleon, when Cleon was at the height of his political influence; only a
few weeks after the play's triumph he was elected general. This turn of
events suggests that, just as Aristophanes was able to abuse and
maltreat Socrates in a comedy without feeling any kind of ill-will
towards him outside the theatre, so Aristophanes' audience could
tolerate and indeed relish the comic abuse and maltreatment of Cleon
without allowing it to influence their political judgement in the Assembly.

This inference can be blocked only if one assumes a significant
difference in political outlook, either between the comic audience
and the voters in the Assembly, or between the judges of the comic
competition and the audience at large. There is nothing to commend
the latter supposition. We do not know by what criteria the Council
drew up its list of potential judges;[14] but we have no reason to suppose
that the procedure was such as would produce results consistently at
variance, politically or indeed aesthetically, with the preferences of
the audience as a whole, and some reason to doubt whether the *demos*
would have tolerated it had it done so. And it is with a consistent
discrepancy that we would have to reckon, since the success of *Knights*
was far from being a freak result; Aristophanes was highly successful

---

[14] For what is known of the procedure see A. W. Pickard-Cambridge, *The
Dramatic Festivals of Athens*[2] (Oxford 1968) 95–8.

in his early career with a whole series of aggressively political comedies.[15] It is worth observing that, although he (naturally enough)
often appeals specifically to the judges for a favourable verdict, Aristophanes never tries to drive a wedge between their verdict and that of
the audience at large; when he is looking back on the failure of
*Clouds,* for example, it is the audience that he blames for the miscarriage of justice (*Wasps* 1016–7, 1043–5, *Clouds* 518–27, cf. *Birds* 445–6).
As for the respective composition of audience and Assembly, we
know so little about either that comparison is difficult. Admission to
the theatre was not free of charge, and this would make it difficult for
the very poorest citizens to attend before the institution of the theoric
fund in the mid-fourth century.[16] But the theatre was substantially
more capacious than the Pnyx, which seems to have seated no more
than six thousand in the fifth century; the use of coercive devices such
as the dyed rope (cf. *Ach.* 21–2) to encourage attendance implies that
the Pnyx was not readily filled in the late fifth century; and the
introduction of payment for attendance at the Assembly in the fourth
century suggests that in the fifth-century its composition, no less than
that of the theatre, would have been weighted against the poorest
citizens.[17] There seems, therefore, to be no good reason for postulat-
ing a significant difference in political outlook between the comic
audience and the Assembly. This accords well with the belief of
pseudo-Xenophon that the *demos* exercised informal control over the
political content of comedy (*Ath.Pol.* 2.18, a passage to which we
shall return). Consequently, the inference must stand that the audience of comedy relished the abuse of leaders whom they nevertheless
continued to support in real political life. Such a conclusion does not
strike me as paradoxical.

----

[15] It was presumably because the passage was particularly well-received at its
original performance that Aristophanes chose to repeat *Wasps* 1030–5 (an abusive
description of Cleon) almost verbatim at *Peace* 752–8.

[16] For the dating see E. Ruschenbusch, *ZPE* 36 (1979) 303–8; P. J. Rhodes, *A
Commentary on the Aristotelian Athenaion Politeia* (Oxford 1981) 514.

[17] On attendance at the Assembly see M. H. Hansen, *GRBS* 17 (1976) 115–34,
and (on payment) *CPh* 74 (1979) 48–9 (= *The Athenian Ecclesia* [Copenhagen 1983]
1–23, 136–7). Note also that a special Assembly was held in the theatre after the
festival to review its conduct (see Pickard-Cambridge [n.14] 68–70).

## 4. Lysistrata

In the case of *Lysistrata* it is possible to apply a third kind of external control, that inferred from the objective circumstances of the play's production. Given Athens' highly unfavourable military situation in 411, no one could have expected Sparta to open negotiations or, if Athens took the initiative, to offer tolerable terms; it is therefore not likely that *Lysistrata* was written to commend peace as a realisable goal in the real world, or that its audience would have understood it in that sense.[18] The very mechanism of the plot shows that the situational constraints were not lost on Aristophanes. In *Acharnians* Spartan readiness to respond favourably to Dicaeopolis' overtures is simply taken for granted; in *Lysistrata*, by contrast, it is necessary to cripple both belligerents before a reconciliation is possible on mutually acceptable terms. It would have been futile to recommend as a real policy the kind of peace which *Lysistrata* envisages, since its realisation presupposed a Spartan willingness to reciprocate which Athens was certainly in no position to secure. On the other hand, the play conveys no hint of support for the only kind of peacemaking policy that was an available option for Athens at this time; there is no suggestion, that is to say, that Athens should open negotiations and allow Sparta to dictate terms. Peace in *Lysistrata*, therefore, is a matter of pure fantasy, and can have no direct bearing on the issues of political debate outside the theatre.[19]

What, then, are we to make of the speech in which the play's peace-making 'policy' is expounded at length (1112–87)? De Ste Croix says of this speech that it is 'completely serious in character and

---

[18] This point is rightly emphasised by H. D. Westlake, *Phoenix* 36 (1980) 38–42; contrast de Ste Croix (n.6) 368, 370.

[19] Newiger recognises that the play's treatment of the war is a 'utopian conception', peace on moderate terms being 'certainly impossible' in 411 (*YCS* 26 [1980] 232–4), and argues that 'the meaning of the play is internal unity and the strengthening of Athens as a precondition for peace with external enemies' (p.236). However, the references to internal politics are hardly the 'central point' of Lysistrata's speech to the Proboulos (574–86 are introduced almost incidentally, to justify the application of domestic analogies to political issues: 566–73); and domestic reconciliation is not otherwise an extensive theme of the play (Newiger points to the reconciliation of the old men and women of the Chorus: but this is a relatively superficial conflict, trivially restored; the fundamental domestic conflict – between wives and men of an age for military service – is a product of the war, and cannot be resolved until peace is made: and Aristophanes significantly does not bother to pursue this theme at the end of the play, but allows it to be displaced by the celebration of external reconciliation).

without a single jest'.[20] That claim is false: it is, after all, Lysistrata
herself who sets the ribald tone of the scene by introducing the
naked Reconciliation (1114 ff.) and by making the indecorous suggestion of 1119;[21] the main part of her speech opens paratragically
(1124-7), and its first section concludes with a tragic line (1135). It
may be true thereafter that Lysistrata's speech is 'without a single
jest';[22] but that, surely, is precisely the joke: Lysistrata adopts an
elevated tone which is hilariously deflated by the background action
(two men with chronic erections are inspecting a naked woman's
anatomy as Lysistrata speaks and, not unnaturally, they show greater
interest in the girl than in what is being said: 1148, 1157-8), by the
ribald interjections which punctuate the speech, and by the culminat-
ing transformation of territorial negotiations into a web of obscene
*doubles entendres*.[23] It is hardly satisfactory, therefore, to treat Lysistrata's speech as if it were (in de Ste Croix's image) serious meat that
could be extracted from a purely external comic sandwich; and while
it is true that serious points can be conveyed in comic guise, it needs to
be shown, not assumed, in each case that something of the kind is
happening.[24] I do not see how that can be shown in the case of *Lys.*
1112-87; the passage makes excellent comic sense without it, as we
have seen. Since we have already found independent reason to doubt
that the peace making in *Lysistrata* is anything other than fantasy, we

---

[20] De Ste Croix (n.6) 368; contrast G. A. H. Chapman, *Acta Classica* 22 (1978)
63-4.

[21] On the tone of σάθη (1119) see N. G. Wilson, *GRBS* 23 (1982) 160. Since we
have remarked on some less dignified aspects of the portrayal of Lysistrata, it might
be appropriate to add a brief comment on D. M. Lewis' theory of her identity. In
*BSA* 60 (1955) 1-12 he showed (a) that Lysistrata did not share her name with the
priestess of Athene Polias, and (b) that Myrrhine did share her name with the
priestess of Athene Nike. Since Myrrhine was an extremely common name the
latter datum is not very striking (and one is entitled to doubt whether Myrrhine the
priestess was in 411 a young wife with an infant child and a suggestively named
husband); thus we are left with (a). I do not myself think that Aristophanes' failure
to give his heroine the priestess's name (he could have done so, had he wished)
legitimates the conclusion that he intended a reference to her.

[22] The Greek orators display such a talent for tendentious distortion of historical
*exempla* (see, for example, Dover, *Greek Popular Morality* [Oxford 1974] 11-13)
that I hesitate to endorse Wilson's suggestion ([n.21] 161) that the distortions of
history in 1138-44, 1150-6 are meant to be perceived as such and found comic; but
that is a possibility.

[23] See J. Henderson, *YCS* 26 (1980) 215 n.110 (where the cross-reference should
read: '*AJP* 95 (1974) 344 ff.').

[24] De Ste Croix (n.6) 357, 360.

need not feel reluctant to conclude that the comedy of the scene in which it is commended was not meant to be a vehicle of serious intent.

## 5. Acharnians

The control which we applied to *Lysistrata* is not available for *Acharnians;* in this case we must depend more exclusively on internal evidence. In his discussion of this play, de Ste Croix lays a good deal of weight on two points about its hero: on his identification with the poet (377–82, 497–505), and on the implications of the name Dicaeopolis.[25] The latter point need not detain us. 'Just City,' as de Ste Croix says, 'does what the city ought to have done': but that we know in any case, for the wisdom of Dicaeopolis' words and actions is a premise of the plot, to which his name therefore adds nothing. The identification of Dicaeopolis with the poet is more interesting, but it is far from obvious that we should read it as a guarantee of serious intent. The lines in which the identification is made suspend the founding pretence of drama ('break the dramatic illusion', as we are forced to say for want of an apt term). This is a very frequent device in Aristophanes, and it is commonly a *humorous* device; why should we suppose otherwise here?

One reason why we might suppose otherwise is that the identification of Dicaeopolis with Aristophanes is closely bound up with the elaborate defensive preparations which Diceaopolis makes for his speech. In the first passage he remarks warily on the fierce temper of his (Dicaeopolis') auditors (370–6) and recalls the attack which Cleon made on him (Aristophanes) after *Babylonians* was performed the previous year (377–82);[26] he decides that he must apply to Euripides for some tear-jerking devices by which to win a sympathetic hearing (383–4, 393–4). Thus this first identification turns out to be an excuse for a long burlesque of Euripides – an outcome which should, perhaps, give pause to those who see in the identification a signal of underlying seriousness. (Dicaeopolis, at least, does not take his forthcoming speech altogether seriously; he admits quite freely in 440–5 that his plan is to make fools of the dim-witted Chorus with his clever

[25] De Ste Croix (n.6) 363–5, 369–70.

[26] It is, I think, Aristophanes rather than Callistratus; see S. Halliwell, *CQ* 30 (1980) 33–45, and (for an opposing view) D. M. MacDowell, *CQ* 32 (1982) 21–6.

Euripidean rhetoric: ῥηματίοις 445, 447; cf. *Clouds* 943.) Suitably at-
tired after his visit to Euripides, Dicaeopolis begins his speech; the
identification is renewed (499–500), and Cleon reappears: 'this is the
Lenaea, so he can't say that I'm slandering the city before foreigners;
and anyway, it's not the city that I'm criticising, but a few good-
for-nothing individuals' (502–8, 515–8). This might seem more serious. But we must not forget that Dicaeopolis' 'suitable attire' constit-
utes a grotesque visual joke; that his account of the war's origins, so
elaborately prepared for, turns out to be utterly preposterous;[27] and
that the speech as a whole is riddled with parody of *Telephus* – its
opening words set the tone.[28] Furnishing this farrago of jokes with
such an elaborate build-up is itself a joke (a form of bathos); but is
even the build-up as serious as it seems at first sight, or is it not
perhaps itself tongue-in-cheek? The obvious possibility that Dicaeopolis' mock-seriousness is in reality part of a joke against Cleon does
not seem to have been considered as carefully as it deserves. We do
not know much about Cleon's prosecution of the poet. Since it was
heard before the Council (379) it was probably an εἰσαγγελία;[29] but
the procedure adopted is of less significance than the outcome: the
prosecution *failed* (381–2). By alluding to the affair here, therefore,
Aristophanes is rubbing his antagonist's nose in the ineffectualness of
his attack.[30] The jibe would have been even more pointed if Aristoph-

---

[27] De Ste Croix wickedly remarks that Dicaeopolis' argument 'nicely represents
the consensus of modern scholarly opinion on the outbreak of the war' ([n.6] 366);
but in saying this he abstracts from the awkward detail of Dicaeopolis' case: most
modern scholars would have doubts about the prostitutes, for example (most but,
astonishingly, not all; MacDowell is quite willing to accept them, though even he
concedes that 'Aspasia's loss of her two girls may not have been the only reason
why Perikles proposed the Megarian decree': see *G&R* 30 [1983] 151–5). For a less
tongue-in-cheek evaluation of the speech see de Ste Croix's comment on p.242:
'what we are being given is a whole series of comic exaggerations, with scarcely an
atom of truth in them'.

[28] Rightly emphasised by W. G. Forrest, *Phoenix* 17 (1963) 8–9 (contrast Mac-
Dowell [n.27] 149–51); but Herodotus is not parodied: C. W. Fornara, *JHS* 91 (1971)
25–34.

[29] See P. J. Rhodes, *The Athenian Boule* (Oxford 1972) 162–71.

[30] I am reminded of the way in which Aristophanes thumbs his nose at Cleon in
*Wasps* 1284–91, where I agree with MacDowell and Sommerstein (*ad loc.*) that
1291 cannot refer to *Knights:* that would be stale; rather the poet is gloating over the
trick he has played on Cleon *in this play.* (In 62–3 Aristophanes claims that he is
going to leave Cleon alone; but that is a bluff, as the audience will realise as soon as
they hear the old man's name at 133–4; the trial scene will not disappoint them. On
133–4, MacDowell is right to note the pause for laughter at this point, but misses

anes could count on the audience's agreeing that the attack was an
inappropriate reaction to a comedy, and I shall argue in due course
that the audience would indeed have inclined to that view. It is also
worth asking why Aristophanes nowhere else thinks it necessary to
construct even remotely similar defences. The obvious answer is that
such a defence was topical only here, in the first play he produced
after the clash with Cleon; but topicality is more usually seen as a
virtue of jokes than of defences seriously intended. I am inclined to
believe, therefore, that Aristophanes' defensive posturing in *Acharnians* is to be understood as a joke at Cleon's expense; that is at any
rate a possible reading, and the case for taking Dicaeopolis' speech
seriously is therefore deprived of its most substantial support.

It is, of course, again a possibility that a serious point is being
conveyed by means of a comic vehicle; but, as always, we must ask
what positive reason there is for supposing that to be so in the given
case. We have found no reason to make that supposition here (or none
that stands up to scrutiny); and the analogy of *Lysistrata* would encourage us to assume that this is because the supposition is in point of
fact false.

## 6. *The Poet as Adviser*

In our discussion of *Acharnians* we have not yet considered its parabasis. This might seem a tendentious omission, since Aristophanes
lays claim in it to the role of political adviser, a claim which, if taken
seriously, would give us some reason for expecting to find serious
intent in Aristophanic comedy, and therefore for regarding more
sympathetically individual alleged instances.[31] But Aristophanes does
not encourage us to take the claim seriously. His attempt to show that
he has benefited the Athenians is in part, at least, a piece of amiable
banter with the audience; to say 'I have stopped you being χαυνοπολῖται' is to say, 'in your natural state that is precisely what you are' (as
we shall see, this kind of light-hearted abuse of the audience is a

---

the point of the joke: 'men are not usually named after the politicians they support';
rather, men are not named 'pro-Cleon' in, of all people, Aristophanes without some
good jokes being in prospect.)

[31] De Ste Croix does not lay any stress on the parabasis (wisely, I think); contrast
MacDowell (n.27) 155–6.

common technique in Aristophanes). It then develops into an amusing fantasy: 'look,' he says, 'the allies are flocking to pay their tribute now, and all because they want to see the Man Who Dared To Tell The Truth In Athens; even the king of Persia has heard of that astonishing feat of daring, and *he* says that I'm a military asset at least as important as the navy; that's why Sparta wants Aegina back – it's not the island they're worried about: they want to get hold of *me*' (643–54). At this point Aristophanes does give one piece of direct advice: do not surrender Aegina to the Spartans (655); since the autonomy of Aegina was one of Sparta's main demands, this is equivalent to advising Athens not to accept Spartan terms. That is part of an elaborate joke, of course, but it is surely not the kind of joke that Aristophanes would have made at this point had he really intended the play to promote a peace-making policy;[32] and it is in any case significant that Aristophanes absorbs the role of adviser so promptly into the realm of the purely comic.

This disarming of the adviser's role is characteristic of Aristophanes' parabases, in which typically he does not offer seriously meant advice to the audience, but plumes himself on his own unique excellence as a comic dramatist (sometimes, as in *Clouds* 537–44, telling bare-faced lies in the process) and invites his Chorus to make bizarre suggestions appropriate to its own fictive persona: the elderly Chorus of *Acharnians*, for example, suggests that old men should be allowed a segregated legal system (713–8); the militant jurors of *Wasps* argue that jury-pay should be reserved for those who have been on active service (1117–21); the Chorus of *Birds* urges upon us the advantages of worshipping the birds instead of the gods (723–36), invites the audience to throw over all civilised restraints and live like the birds (752–68), and points out how useful we would find it if we could grow wings (785–800).[33]

There is one exception to this general tendency. Aristophanes begins the parabasis of *Frogs* by reasserting the role of adviser (686–7; this is his most direct claim to the role), and goes on to urge an amnesty for those disfranchised for their part in the oligarchic coup of 411 (688–705). This was a practicable policy in 405; an amnesty was

---

[32] As Forrest observes ([n.28] 4). (His use of the term 'pacifist' here was injudicious, as de Ste Croix insists; but that is a point of little consequence.)

[33] For an analysis of the contents of the parabasis (with some rather over-confident references to fragments) see G. M. Sifakis, *Parabasis and Animal Choruses* (London 1971) 37–44.

in fact granted later in the same year.[34] Moreover, the passage does seem, by the criterion of jokelessness, a good candidate for the ascription of serious intent. (The antepirrhema, 718–37, does not meet that criterion so well, consisting as it does of a wittily extended metaphorical development of what was, as we shall see, a stock joke in contemporary comedy.) The passage is certainly striking; but it is striking not least for being unique in extant Aristophanes, and it would therefore be an unreliable basis for generalisation about the adviser's role in his work. Furthermore, it does not seem possible to pursue its apparent seriousness beyond the context of the parabasis, where it is explicitly marked; that is, the action of *Frogs* as a whole does not seem to have been designed to convey a comparably serious point. It is true that, when all other tests have proved inconclusive (1411–3),[35] Dionysus tries to break the deadlock by asking the two tragedians to submit samples of the advice they would give to the city (1418–21): what should be done about Alcibiades? How can the city be saved? But it is Euripides whose advice echoes that of the parabasis (1446–50, cf. 718–37); Aeschylus' advice (1463–5) is a blatant anachronism, wholly irrelevant to the actual situation of Athens in 405. If Aeschylus is adjudged the winner, this is not because Aristophanes has made him the better political adviser;[36] it is because he belongs to the 'good old

---

[34] This measure, proposed by Patrocleides, was adopted in the face of the terminal crisis which followed the defeat at Aegospotami (Andocides 1.73–80). Since the Athenians were not willing to implement the policy which Aristophanes commends before then, we might tentatively infer (a) that in commending it Aristophanes was going against the trend of Athenian opinion, and (b) that, if Dicaearchus was right in thinking (i) that *Frogs* was voted a second performance and (ii) that this was because of its parabasis (neither point can be regarded as certain) then this was probably not until the democratic restoration of 403; this is argued by J. T. Allen, *Univ. California Publications in Classical Philology* 11 (1930/3) 143–61; but his arguments are not uniformly strong.

[35] One of the tests is that of didactic effect. Both poets accept that the poet has an educative function (1009–10, 1030–6, 1054–6); Euripides claims to have made the Athenians more alert and intellectually sharper (910, 954–79), while Aeschylus replies that in so doing his rival has undermined the moral and martial excellences that his own plays had instilled (1010–88). This (traditional) view of the poet's function is obviously related to the pose of adviser which Aristophanes sometimes adopts; but that does not tell us whether he takes (or wants his audience to take) the pose seriously on any given occasion (and the function is treated in a burlesque spirit in this scene).

[36] Sommerstein denies that Aeschylus' advice is anachronistic (*CQ* 25 [1974] 24–7); I am unpersuaded. But even if his point is allowed, Aeschylus' advice is banal (with the Spartan army in occupation of Decelea and a Spartan fleet operating in the Aegean, Athens could hardly follow any other strategy than the one which

days', which are bound to win out in the end in comedy (for reasons to be discussed shortly), and because it leads to a splendid comic climax in which Euripides' increasingly desperate protests are countered by the citation of increasingly outrageous paradoxes from his own plays (1471, 1475, 1477–8). Thus the action of *Frogs* is a comic fantasy that Aristophanes has not tried to coordinate with the apparently serious advice of its parabasis, just as the apparently comic advice in the parabasis of *Acharnians* has not been coordinated with the peace-making fantasy of that play's action.[37]

## 7. *Corporate Abuse*

In the parabasis of *Acharnians* the poet's adviserly role is brought into close connection with his abusive function. At first he says only: 'they say that I insult the city and *demos*, but in fact you should be grateful for all the good I've done you' (630–3, 641); but it becomes obvious quite quickly that it is *by* insulting the *demos* that he has (or claims to have) done them good: 'the king of Persia says that whichever side I insult will be greatly improved thereby, and is sure to win the war' (646–51). To be a ξύμβουλος therefore, is (in part, at least) to be abusive, εἰπεῖν κακὰ πολλά.[38] The theory behind this is explained in *Eccl.* 677–80: if children sing the praises of brave men and lampoon cowards at the communal meals of post-revolutionary Athens, the cowards will be ashamed to show their faces, and socially undesirable behaviour will be discouraged.[39] That passage refers to abuse of individuals, to which we shall return; for the present I wish to concentrate on corporate abuse of the kind mentioned in the parabasis of *Acharnians*. (In what

---

Aeschylus, on this view, commends), while Euripides' advice is radical and – if the parabasis is serious – in agreement with Aristophanes' own advice to Athens; so it is hard to see how Aeschylus' advice could be thought, in extradramatic terms, superior.

[37] Compare, for example, the uncoordinated attitudes to father-beating in the parabasis of *Birds* (755–9) and the main action (1337–71); the opportunist use of Socrates' novel theology in *Clouds* (a joke in the early scenes and a source of 'outrage' at the end); the inconsistency between the lyric at *Knights* 1111–50 and the action of the play (cf. 1335–57; see Dover, *Aristophanic Comedy* [London 1972] 98–9).

[38] See Dover (n.22) 23–30.

[39] R. G. Ussher *ad loc.* thinks that epic recitation is in question; but I find κεῖ τις δειλὸς γεγένηται difficult on that view.

follows 'the audience' must be taken to refer to the adult male citizens present.)[40]

In parabases μέμφεσθαι is a recurrent word: the old men blame the city (Ach. 676); the poet blames the audience (Wasps 1016, cf. Clouds 518ff.); the Clouds blame the audience, too, and also pass on a complaint from the Moon (Clouds 576, 608ff.); the women blame the men (Thesm. 831). But one also finds direct abuse of the audience outside the parabasis, combined with humorous violations of 'dramatic illusion': 'look at the audience,' one character will say to another, 'they are all perverts (Clouds 1096–1104), parricides and perjurers (Frogs 274–6), or rascals, thieves and sycophants (Eccl. 433–40)'; or else the audience will be addressed directly: 'you are mad (Peace 55), much nastier at close quarters than you looked from the air – and you looked pretty nasty then (Peace 821–3); and you are exceedingly stupid (Clouds 1201–3).' This is all in a light-hearted vein, of course; the poet evidently enjoys a jocular and amiably disrespectful relationship with his audience (and doubtless the audience enjoyed it as well). But it is important to realise that such jokes are continuous with the kind of indirect abuse implicit in the unflattering representation of groups with whom the audience is effectively identified. For example, since it is the adult male citizens among those present in the theatre who make up the 'real' audience, the audience is effectively equivalent to the demos, and so to the Assembly. Thus when the Assembly is portrayed as a flock of sheep (Wasps 31–6; cf. Knights 749–55), this amounts not to 'they are stupid' (as might a comparable joke about Parliament), but to 'you are stupid.'

That is an almost parenthetic joke; but often enough an equally derogatory view of the demos is a crucial premise of the main action of a play. Knights is a particularly lurid example, but Acharnians also illustrates the point well; in the Assembly-scene we see precisely Sosias's sheep-like gathering, herded in with the dyed rope to sit unprotesting while profiteers fleece and impostors make fools of them, and while the one man among them with any sense is suppressed and ignored. It is presumably to a similar scene that Aristophanes alludes in the parabasis when he claims that his abuse has

---

[40] Metics and (at the Dionysia) non-residents were present (Ach. 503–9), as well as minors and (perhaps) some women (see Pickard-Cambridge [n.14] 263–5; Wilson [n.21] 158–9 presents the case against women). But the adult citizens formed the *effective* audience: others may have been present, but they were the ones addressed. Thus in Ach. 507ff. 'we' are contrasted with the metic 'they', and in the parabasis τὸ θέατρον is treated as equivalent to the Athenian demos.

stopped the Athenians being χαυνοπολῖται and made them wise to the insidious deceits of toadying allied ambassadors (633–40). Observe that Aristophanes is here claiming credit on the grounds that his abuse has stopped the audience doing essentially the very thing that he has just abusively portrayed them as still doing; this inconsistency (another instance of parabasis and action being uncoordinated)[41] should give pause to those who think that his unflattering portrait of the state of Athenian political life has a serious critical edge. In fact, we are dealing with a comic stereotype for which only the most tenuous attachment to reality can safely be assumed. After all, Aristophanes again and again devised plots which assume that Athens is in the most desperate of straits: in *Acharnians* and *Wasps* public life is so insane that sensible individuals must withdraw into a purely private world; in *Lysistrata* and *Ecclesiazusae* things are so bad that only (of all improbable things) a *coup d'état* by the women can introduce some sense; in *Knights, Frogs* and *Wealth* even more far-fetched devices are required to put things right. If Aristophanes really felt so desperate throughout his career, it is astonishing that he could write such funny plays. But of course he did not; he chose to portray Athens in this unflattering light because his audience, *knowing it to be untrue* (for they certainly were not in the throes of despair throughout his career), laughed when he did so. They seem to have laughed when his rivals did so, as well; Eupolis brought Solon, Miltiades, Aristides and Pericles back from the dead in the *Demes* of 412.

The comic opportunism apparent in the discrepancies between parabasis and action will also be in evidence if we consider Aristophanes' treatment of the position from which his abuse of the audience is launched. Given the retrospective cast of Greek culture, from Homer's depreciation of 'men as they are now' to the fifth-century reformers and revolutionaries who adopted the 'ancestral constitution' as their slogan,[42] to abuse the present-day world was to adopt a conservative standpoint; even the highly novel constitutional innovation envisaged in *Ecclesiazusae* is justified by reference to the conservatism of women (*Eccl.* 214–28). So *Knights* ends triumphantly with the transformation of the degenerate Demos into his old self, the 'violet-crowned' Athens of old, city of Aristides and Miltiades, of the

---

[41] Thus I cannot accept the approach to the parabasis of *Ach.* urged by A. M. Bowie, *CQ* 32 (1982) 27–40; a similar attempt to integrate incidental lyrics in C. Moulton, *Aristophanic Poetry* (Hypomnemata 68, Göttingen 1981) 18–47, strikes me as equally unsuccessful (contrast n.37 above; and see further the Appendix).

[42] See M. I. Finley, *The Use and Abuse of History* (London 1975) 34–59.

trophy at Marathon (*Knights* 1323, 1325, 1333–4); in *Lysistrata* the
fantasy of peace envisages a return (scarcely possible in 411, whatever was felt in the euphoric days of 421: cf. *Peace* 1080–2) to the
Cimonian dual hegemony (*Lys.* 1128–56); in *Frogs* it is Aeschylus, the
poet of old Athens, who is brought back to life, just as in Eupolis'
*Demes* it is the politicians of old Athens who return to put things
right.

But even in Praxagora's speech in *Ecclesiazusae* the conservative
standpoint is not treated with complete respect; the examples she
cites of women continuing to act κατὰ τὸν ἀρχαῖον νόμον are all trivial,
and most play on the comic cliché that women are hopelessly addic-
ted to drink and sex. Notoriously Aristophanes pokes fun at the old at
the very same time that he uses it to satirise the new: Aeschylus is
treated as iconoclastically as Euripides in *Frogs*, and the conservative
'right argument' in *Clouds* is mercilessly handled; as for the 'brave old
men of Marathon', they are, as Gomme observed, 'invariably on the
wrong side, or *are* the wrong side'.[43] Thus the exaltation of the 'good
old days' is a conventional and inevitable stance for the comic poet
who wishes to abuse his contemporary audience, but it does not
provide Aristophanes with a stable programmatic platform; instead
he uses it opportunistically, launching his shafts against the present
day from it when he sees fit, but as readily turning his weapons against
it if that will raise a laugh. Here too, therefore, we find reason to doubt
a 'serious' thrust either in the direct abuse or in the indirectly abusive
portrayal of audience and *demos*; here too the poet's adviserly role
has been absorbed into a realm of fantasy and pure comedy.

## 8. *Individual Abuse*

Aristophanes does not abuse only his audience and its equivalents *en
masse*, but also singles out individual members of the community for
mockery; to what end? Mockery can serve a number of different
functions.[44] On one level it is a communally applied sanction; the fear
of mockery, and of the consequent loss of standing in the community,
discourages deviant behaviour (this is the principle underlying *Eccl.*

---

[43] Gomme (n.1) 99.

[44] For this, as for many other aspects of fifth-century Athenian society, J. du
Boulay's *Portrait of a Greek Mountain Village* (Oxford 1974) provides an illumi-
nating model; see esp. pp. 181–7.

677–80, cited above; cf. *Knights* 1274–5). It is also a weapon that individuals can use in the competition for superior standing in the community, and above all in political competition; this function is very evident in the Greek orators.[45] A scrupulous respect for the truth is not to be expected in such a case; Demosthenes and Aeschines did not necessarily believe the slurs they cast on each other's ancestry, private life and public integrity, or expect their audience to believe them. Rather, by distorting the known facts in an unfavourable way, or even by inventing 'facts', so long as the inventions have some recognisably apt point of attachment to the victim, a speaker can raise a laugh at his opponent's expense, inflicting on him a loss of face and so subverting the audience's capacity to give his case their serious attention (cf. Gorgias' precept τὴν μὲν σπουδὴν διαφθείρειν τῶν ἐναντίων γέλωτι: Ar.*Rhet.* 1419b4–5); and to win an exchange of insults by superior skill is to establish one level of argumentative superiority over him, and so to detract from the overall effect of the presentation of his case.

But abuse can also be transformed into entertainment, or even into a form of art; and in such a case mockery can be detached, not only from any commitment to veracity, but also from any hostile intent towards the victim (although this is not necessarily absent). As West comments on the 'marvellous rudeness' of Theognis 453–6, 'it is the perfection of its form, rather than the justice of its sentiment, that invites applause':[46]

> ὤνθρωπ', εἰ γνώμης ἔλαχες μέρος ὥσπερ ἀνοίης
> καὶ σώφρων οὕτως ὥσπερ ἄφρων ἐγένου,
> πολλοῖς ἂν ζηλωτὸς ἐφαίνεο τῶνδε πολιτῶν
> οὕτως ὥσπερ νῦν οὐδενὸς ἄξιος εἶ.

West plausibly suggests as a context for these lines 'that abusive banter which was exchanged in song by young men at feasts', citing *hHerm.* 55 f. and other evidence for symposiastic improvisation, which (as West says) 'in such convivial circumstances is naturally liable to veer in the direction of badinage'.[47]

---

[45] See Dover (n.22) 30–3. (In *Knights* the exchanges between the Paphlagonian and the sausage-seller serve, with admirable economy, both to generate abuse of Cleon and to parody this aspect of political competition.)

[46] M. L. West, *Studies in Greek Elegy and Iambus* (Berlin & New York 1974) 16.

[47] The abusive comparisons which Philocleon and Lysistratus exchange in *Wasps* 1308–13 show a certain structural similarity to the 'sounds' discussed by W. Labov

The symposiastic context of these last instances calls to mind an anecdote concerning Socrates recorded by Plutarch. Asked whether he was not annoyed by his maltreatment in comedy, Socrates is said to have replied: μὰ Δί' οὐκ ἔγωγε· ὡς γὰρ ἐν συμποσίῳ μεγάλῳ ἐν θεάτρῳ σκώπτομαι (Plut. *de lib. educ.* 10cd). Socrates is not here explaining the conventions of Old Comedy to an 'outsider'; his remark (if authentic, which there is no reason to suppose) is worth quoting only if it is regarded as in some way an extraordinary reaction to comic abuse, if Socrates shows in it a degree of tolerance unusual in the victims of comedy. That would be comprehensible. The experience of witty badinage in a small circle of intimates is rather painless; before a mass audience, especially in a society that placed so high a value on τιμή, mockery would potentially be much more wounding, and would be so whether or not it was inspired by any specifically hostile intent. For the victim to react, as the Socrates of Plutarch's anecdote reacts, with amused equanimity, could be seen as an ideally appropriate reaction to such non-hostile abuse in the theatre, but one which perhaps was infrequently achieved in fifth-century Athens.

But its infrequency should not be exaggerated. We deduced from *Symposium* that Aristophanes' circle of friends included people he had or in due course would make fun of on the stage; and it might in any case seem improbable that comic poets would indulge so freely in abuse if that would have earned them the bitter enmity of large numbers of their social peers, of the men potentially most dangerous as personal enemies. In Athens (as in most places at most times) inability to take a joke tolerantly was socially unacceptable behaviour: οἱ δὲ μήτ' αὐτοὶ ἂν εἰπόντες μηδὲν γελοῖον τοῖς τε λέγουσι δυσχεραίνοντες ἄγροικοι καὶ σκληροὶ δοκοῦσιν εἶναι (Ar.*EN* 1128a7–8). In *Frogs* 367–8 Aristophanes alleges that a politician[48] who had proposed a reduction

---

in 'Rules for ritual insults', *Language in the Inner City* (Oxford 1977) 297–353. Most of the company enjoy the game (ἀνεκρότησαν 1314), but it imports a vulgar tone into the proceedings, and Theophrastus maintains a disdainful *hauteur*; this irritates Philocleon, who deviates from the 'ritualised' frame to make what are, in consequence, highly offensive remarks about each of his fellow guests in turn (1316–21; cf. Xen. *Symp.* 6.8–10). In 'sounds' an insult too near to the truth loses its ritualised character and becomes insulting; conversely, for the victim to protest at or deny a 'sound' (to treat it *as* insulting) is implicitly to concede its nearness to the truth. A similar convention perhaps underlies *Wasps* 1224–30; Cleon's angry reaction is in effect an admission that he is 'a scoundrel and a thief' since, if he were not, he would have been able to accept the charge as mere banter.

[48] Unnamed; Archinus and/or Agyrrhius according to a scholion *ad loc.* (= Plato Com. fr. 133, Sannyrio fr. 9).

in the honorarium paid to comic poets was motivated by resentment, κωμῳδηθείς. The allegation was doubtless a scurrilous lie; but the fact that Aristophanes could use it mockingly implies that resentment of and indirect retaliation against comic poets was seen as absurd and improper. I argued earlier that references to Cleon's prosecution of the poet in *Acharnians* should similarly be read as mocking in tone. Certainly the comic poets seem to have thrown out with impunity claims that in everyday life would have laid them open to prosecution for slander; attempts to impose legal restraints on comedy, for which we have tantalisingly shadowy evidence,[49] were at best short-lived and ineffective. Thus the comic poets seem to have enjoyed, in practice at least, a special license to abuse. This freedom may have been protected by the religious context of the dramatic competition. Aristotle recommends a complete exclusion of αἰσχρολογία and similar indecency from the city, but has to accept religiously sanctioned mockery: εἰ μὴ παρά τισι θεοῖς τοιούτοις οἷς καὶ τὸν τωθασμὸν ἀποδίδωσιν ὁ νόμος (*Pol.* 1336b3–23, cf. *EN* 1128a30–1; he suggests that young people should be excluded from comedy, the presence of adult males satisfying the religious obligation on behalf of women and children). It is presumably for this reason that Aristophanes, in mocking the politician of *Frogs* 367–8, specifies κωμῳδηθεὶς ἐν ταῖς πατρίοις τελεταῖς ταῖς τοῦ Διονύσου; by emphasising the grounds of his license to slander he emphasises the impropriety of the (alleged) *faux pas*.

I would suggest, therefore (and if this is correct, it again illustrates how the poet's potentially critical role as adviser had largely been absorbed into pure comedy in the late fifth century), that the abuse of individuals in Aristophanes can best be seen as a form of entertainment, not indeed unduly concerned to avoid wounding the victim (cf. Ar.*EN* 1128a6–7), but compatible with the absence of offence and not (in general) inspired by any specifically hostile intent, to be evaluated more for its wit and ingenuity than for veracity or even verisimilitude. This last point is not easy to illustrate, since we are so often dependent on Aristophanes (or, worse, on scholiasts themselves tacitly dependent on Aristophanes) for our knowledge of his victims. We shall consider his treatment of Cleon in this light shortly; for the present

---

[49] In the scholia to *Ach.* 67 (which appears to be using a trustworthy source) and *Birds* 1297 (which does not); see A. Körte, *RE* XI 1233–6; S. Halliwell, *CQ* 34 (1984) 86–7 (this article, and the same author's 'Aristophanic satire', *Yearbook of English Studies* 14 [1984] 6–20, are valuable contributions to our understanding of personal abuse in Aristophanes).

Cleonymus and his shield may afford one, necessarily conjectural, illustration.

The artistry of abuse could scarcely be seen to better advantage than in the string of ingenious variations which Aristophanes devises on this theme: see Clouds 353-4 (why do the Clouds look like deer? They've seen Cleonymus the ῥίψασπις); Wasps 15-27 (a bird snatches up a snake and then turns into Cleonymus, who of course drops his ἀσπίς; this initiates a series of jokes, concluding with an obscene pun on ὅπλα); Wasps 818-23 (how does Cleonymus resemble Lycus? He's a hero without any ὅπλα); Peace 670-8 (Cleonymus is a brave man, but of uncertain paternity: when he's in the army he becomes ἀποβολιμαῖος τῶν ὅπλων); Peace 1295-1304 (the child who persists in singing warlike songs turns out to be Lamachus' son; so Trygaeus sends instead for Cleonymus' son, who sings Archilochus: ἄσπιδι μὲν Σαΐων τις ἀγάλ-λεται...); Birds 288-90 ('what's that bird called?' 'A gobbler.' 'You mean it's Cleonymus?' 'Can't be; it hasn't thrown away its crest.'); Birds 1470-81 (the Cleonymus-tree: in autumn it sheds its shields).[50] But what was the truth behind all this? As early as Knights 1372 there seems to be something funny about Cleonymus and his shield; but that passage is curiously unspecific by comparison with later develop-ments, and it suggests a context of evasion of service rather than of desertion in the field. Conjecture may be futile; but one should think rather of an embarrassing mishap than of a criminal act of cowardice as the origin of the joke: perhaps he was excused from some duty for which he had been called up because a fault was found in his equip-ment at the last moment (his shield-strap, for which πόρπαξ is a pompously elevated word, becoming detached, let us say). That would mean that something in essence as innocuous as Pantacles' parade-ground ineptness (Frogs 1036-8) lay behind the subsequent series of jokes, something which was subjected to comic distortion, and which was funny in part because it was a distortion of a harmless absurdity; if Cleonymus had really thrown his shield away, a crime punishable by disfranchisement (Andocides 1.74, and MacDowell ad loc.), it might not have been seen as a laughing matter.[51]

---

[50] See also Wasps 592, Peace 444-6, Eupolis fr.100 Austin=352 KA, and the scholion to Clouds 353. (The joke in Birds 288-90 alludes to the other joke against Cleonymus, his gluttony; see MacDowell on Wasps 19 for further references.)

[51] Sommerstein offers a similar conjecture about Knights 1372 (ad loc.), but does not connect it with the subsequent series of shield-jokes, which he thinks may have been derived from the retreat after Delium (on Wasps 19); but it is uneconomical to assume that Cleonymus' shield became funny twice, and easy to suspect that some one trivial incident has been comically inflated.

## 9. Rich and Poor

We have already commented on de Ste Croix's account of Aristophanes' attitude to the war; in this section I shall consider his remarks on Aristophanes' use of social and political terminology, on his treatment of the rich as a class, and on his leniency towards certain public figures, stimulating remarks that are, nevertheless, almost completely misleading.[52]

De Ste Croix conveys the impression that evaluative words like χρηστός and πονηρός, and above all the term καλὸς κἀγαθός, typically carry social, and indeed somewhat restrictive social, implications in Aristophanes; 'Aristophanes' *kaloi kagathoi* have an unmistakably social and political character almost every time they are mentioned'.[53] It is true that Aristophanes sometimes uses the words demonstrably in this sense. In other passages the context does not dictate our interpretation of the words; in these passages, although the social connotation is in principle available, it would be arbitrary to assume that it is intended, for there are also passages for which this interpretation can be ruled out.[54] In *Clouds* 101, for example, Strepsiades describes the occupants of the 'thinkery' as μεριμνοσοφισταὶ καλοί τε κἀγαθοί. Obviously he does not mean that Socrates and his friends are aristocrats (not true of Socrates, and in any case irrelevant), but that they are good *qua* sophists, good of their kind; they are the best merimnosophists that money can buy. When χρηστός or καλὸς κἀγαθός are applied to πολίτης, the meaning is similarly 'good *qua* citizen'; and the criteria of excellence for a citizen in Aristophanes do not as a rule include wealth and aristocratic breeding. Dicaeopolis is a πολίτης χρηστός because of his responsible behaviour as an ordinary citizen (*Ach.* 595-7; cf. *Peace* 910), just as in *Thesm.* 830-43 the ἀνὴρ χρηστός is the man who serves the city well (ταξίαρχον ἢ στρατηγόν 833, cf. 839 τὸν ἀνδρεῖον), while the ἀνὴρ πονηρός is the man who discharges his

---

[52] De Ste Croix (n.6) 358-62, 371-6.

[53] De Ste Croix (n.6) 374, cf. 359. Sommerstein concurs: 'In his fifth-century plays ... as has been shown (in my view conclusively) by de Ste Croix, Aristophanes reveals himself as one who instinctively speaks the language and thinks the thoughts of the well-to-do' (*CQ* 34 [1984] 314); since I disagree with this conclusion, I do not share the puzzlement which Sommerstein feels over the politics of Aristophanes' fourth-century plays.

[54] Demonstrably social: e.g. *Knights* 185-6, 735, 738-40; indeterminate: e.g. *Lys.* 1059-60; moral rather than social: e.g. *Knights* 1274-5 (shown by 1276-89, contrasting Arignotus with his πονηρός brother), *Lys.* 350-1; further references in text (note also Phrynichus fr. 59, Eupolis fr. 118=129).

duty badly (who may be a rich man: τριήραρχον 837, cf. *Frogs* 1065–6).
A case less easy to decide is *Knights* 225–8: 'there are a thousand
knights, ἄνδρες ἀγαθοί, who hate Cleon, and they will help you, and
the καλοὶ κἀγαθοί among the citizens, and anyone who is δεξιός among
the spectators'. Protesting against Gomme's claim that in 227 καλὸς
κἀγαθός is used in a moral sense, de Ste Croix argues: 'in fact all the
people who are being referred to in lines 225–8 are by definition those
who are political opponents of Cleon, and of course Aristophanes
feels able to take it for granted that all *kaloi kagathoi* are anti-Cleon!
The real force of the expression here is therefore social and political,
and any moral implications are purely consequential upon that'.[55]
The real point, however, is not whether all καλοὶ κἀγαθοί are anti-
Cleon, but whether all those who are anti-Cleon are καλοὶ κἀγαθοί in
the restricted social sense. 'Demosthenes' is trying to encourage the
sausage-seller by pointing to the *breadth* of support for him, and will
hardly wish therefore to *restrict* the application of καλὸς κἀγαθός to a
small subsection of Athenian society. Rather he is saying: the Chorus
will support you, and all decent ordinary people (like Dicaeopolis:
*Ach.* 595–7), and the clever spectators (and who in the audience will
not want to be clever?).[56] Thus καλὸς κἀγαθός here is (in terms of de
Ste Croix's classification) a 'Group C' usage, in which 'the connotation of *kalos kagathos* is ... predominantly moral: uprightness of
character, or the quality of being a patriotic and good citizen'.[57] In
*Wealth* χρηστός has this moral sense almost without exception; it is
associated with a whole string of positive moral terms and applied to
poor men like Chremylus, while the rich are condemned as πονηροί
and endowed with all manner of vices.[58] There is only one passage in
*Wealth* in which χρηστός has a restricted social sense, and that is

---

[55] De Ste Croix (n.6) 374, citing Gomme, *CQ* 3 (1953) 66–7.

[56] De Ste Croix's comment on this last line (228) is nothing short of perverse: 'cf.,
for δεξιός Ps.-Xen., *Ath.Pol.* 1.6,9' ([n.6] 360); cf., rather, *Knights* 233, and frequently
in Aristophanes.

[57] De Ste Croix (n.6) 375. (Not only καλὸς κἀγαθός acquires this wide extension;
εὐγενής is applied in *Thesm.* 330–1 to all free Athenian women.)

[58] The poor man is χρηστός (92–3, 386, 490, 497, 503, 826 [cf. 829 ff.], 977), δίκαιος
(28, 89, 94, 97, 219, 475, 751), θεοσεβής (28, cf. 497), εὔορκος (61), σοφός and κόσμιος
(89), δεξιός and σώφρων (387), ἀγαθός (495). The rich are πονηροί (31, 96, 491, 496,
502, 781, 862, 869, 939, 957), ἄδικοι (37, cf. 755), ἄθεοι (491, 496), μοχθηροί (109),
πανοῦργοι (37), ἱερόσυλοι, ῥήτορες and συκοφάνται (30–1, cf. 850ff.), τοιχωρύχοι (869,
909, 939). The sycophant claims to be φιλόπολις καὶ χρηστός (900, a significant
combination), but his claim is naturally rejected on the grounds that he does
nothing useful (901, 909–10; cf. 939 πονηρὸν ἄνδρα καὶ τοιχωρύχον).

ironical, a barbed reference to the mercenary sexual μοχθηρία of young
gentlemen (153–9).[59]

It is clear from the references collected in n.58 that *Wealth* takes a
somewhat unfavourable view of the rich; de Ste Croix says that the
'unflattering references to the rich' in this play are few, which is
untrue (as we have seen), and that they are demanded by the plot,
which is true but unhelpful since the same could be said of the
sympathetic treatment of the rich in *Knights*, on which in the same
context de Ste Croix lays considerable emphasis.[60] In fact de Ste Croix
there seriously misrepresents the range of attitudes displayed towards
the rich in Aristophanes' plays. Consider first the passages that he
alleges as 'sympathetic'. *Knights* 1137–40: the παχεῖς here are the
thieving politicians Demos fattens for slaughter, the last people in the
world with whom Aristophanes will sympathise; *Knights* 223–4: this
is simply a polar expression ('the rich fear him and the poor are
terrified of him' = 'everyone is afraid of him') and evinces no special
sympathy for any one class; *Knights* 264–5: this is sympathetic, but
the sympathy is evoked by the victim's helpless naivete (ἀμνοκῶν …
καὶ μὴ πονηρὸς καὶ τρέμων τὰ πράγματα; note that πονηρός here is moral)
more than by his wealth; *Eccl.* 197–8: unsympathetic, for the πλούσιοι
and the farmers in opposing the construction of warships are subor-
dinating national security to their private financial advantage, just as
the *demos* as a whole prefers public pay to ship-building (*Knights*
1351–6; cf. *Eccl.* 205–8).[61] This leaves very little: *Peace* 639–40, and
two passages in *Wasps* (288–9, 626–7) which will bear closer scrutiny.

First it should be stressed that the theme of rich and poor is not
particularly prominent in the 'juridical' portion of this play (see 241,
287, 464, 575, 627). It is true that the pleasure Philocleon takes in
convicting or humiliating any defendant is enhanced when the defendant is wealthy (575, 626–7); but equally he enjoys exercising
power over the physically imposing (553) and the politically influential (592–3, 596–600) – in short, it is the deference of anyone to whom
he might normally have to defer that he relishes. Further, are the

---

[59] De Ste Croix (n.6) 375 claims that καλὸς κἀγαθός is never used by Aristophanes
in a hostile context, marked by sarcasm or irony; this *may* be true of καλὸς κἀγαθός,
but it is not true of χρηστός (we shall see further instances below), nor of the noun
καλοκἀγαθία (fr. 198.8=205) – which may prompt doubts about the adjective in, e.g.,
*Wasps* 1256.

[60] De Ste Croix (n.6) 360–1.

[61] Note that μισθοφορία is not a passion only of the lower classes: *Ach.* 65–7,
595–619, etc.

references to rich victims really sympathetic? Two factors qualify or cancel any such sympathy. First, although the audience knows abstractly that Philocleon is in the wrong and wants Bdelycleon to win the argument, they are likely to find him a sympathetic and engaging character;[62] thus the audience is invited into a kind of complicity with him and *enjoys* his triumph over the rich, the strong and the powerful. Secondly, it is a standing assumption in Aristophanes that politicians are on the make; hence it can safely be taken for granted that the rich victims of Philocleon and his colleagues are guilty. This point is vividly illustrated by the case of Laches, the first rich victim mentioned in the play (240–1), who is subsequently metamorphosed into Labes, the defendant dog in the household trial. De Ste Croix believes that 'Labes-Laches is sympathetically treated by Aristophanes (see esp. *Wasps* 952–72) and acquitted (994)'.[63] In fact he is sympathetically treated by *Bdelycleon* – not surprisingly, since Bdelycleon is counsel for the defence – and is acquitted only because Bdelycleon is determined to break Philocleon's obsession by trickery; that Philocleon for his part would have convicted the defendant solely out of prejudice and professional pride is true, but does not alter the fact that the dog is patently guilty (not even Bdelycleon denies that, and if you doubt it just look at his name; cf. 836–8). Laches is turned into a dog, mocked and condescended to, written off as beyond dispute guilty of malfeasance: 'sympathetically treated'!

We have already seen how the assumption that the rich are invariably corrupt underlies the plot of *Wealth*; in that same play one finds also an expression of the ideology of the poor. It must be emphasised here that πένης means 'poor', not in the sense 'very poor' or 'destitute', but as 'not rich'; Poverty (πενία) is sharply distinguished from her 'sister' Penury (πτωχεία). The poor man, in this sense, has no significant surplus, but nor does he go short (548–54); his existence, frugal and hard-working (551), is the mother both of invention, of all crafts and skills (527–34), and of the moral virtues: wealth debauches and degrades (558–61, 563–4). So it is that politicians do right by the city and *demos* when they are poor, but once they have enriched themselves at public expense they lose their integrity and turn against the *demos* (567–70).[64] It is true that Poverty, who makes these claims, is

[62] Cf. Dover (n.37) 125–7.

[63] De Ste Croix (n.6) 367.

[64] The approval of poor politicians in this passage sits uncomfortably with the view that Aristophanes takes a consistently hostile attitude to the political influence of the 'lower orders'.

driven off the stage ignominiously; but Chremylus does not try to *refute* her arguments, or even listen to them seriously (as she complains in 557).[65] The rebuff of Poverty means only that, as so often in Aristophanes, mere facts have not been allowed to interfere with wishful fantasy; facts they nevertheless are, as Chremylus himself and his fellows, just, pious and decent (n. 58), thrifty without stinginess (245-9), and hard workers to a man (223-4, 254), will suffice to prove. Poverty's doctrine is more in keeping with the premises of the plot than is its scornful rejection by Chremylus.

Chremylus and his fellows are of the middle rank of society, neither rich nor destitute; *Wealth* therefore provides the analogy to Euripides' exaltation of οἱ ἐν μέσῳ (E.Su.238-45) which de Ste Croix misses in Aristophanes.[66] It should not surprise us to find the ideology of this class expressed in comedy. As has often been pointed out, Aristophanes' heroes are typically men of precisely that rank; Dicaeopolis, Strepsiades (before his son ran up huge debts, and with admitted qualifications on the moral side) and Trygaeus are, like Chremylus, farmers working their own land, neither destitute nor positively wealthy, πολῖται χρηστοί. The very rich in fact appear rather rarely in the plays, and Strepsiades' autobiographical reflections indicate the gulf which separates him from the very wealthy strata of society in which his wife originated. In consequence the rich are often mentioned in comedy in terms suggesting a 'they' whose mannerisms are regarded with a certain disapproval. This is true of Strepsiades' wife, the niece of Megacles son of Megacles, σεμνὴν, τρυφῶσαν, ἐγκεκοισυρωμένην (*Clouds* 48, cf. 51-5, 61, 67-70); and Coesyra, who for Strepsiades epitomises aristocratic luxuriousness (*Clouds* 48, 800), appears also in *Ach.* 614, significantly in a context in which Dicaeopolis is trying to excite resentment against the elite who draw public pay for easy jobs while the ordinary folk of the Chorus endure hardship (*Ach.* 599-619). Elsewhere, when young men are satirised for their fashionable vices and affectations it is of course *rich* young men who are in mind.[67]

---

[65] Note the opposition of σκώπτειν καὶ κωμῳδεῖν to σπουδάζειν. Chremylus' essentially frivolous attitude is shown in 555-6, 562, 565, where he continues simply to ignore the distinction between poverty and penury, the vices of 565 properly attaching to the latter (as well as to wealth: n.58 above).

[66] De Ste Croix (n.6) 360.

[67] *Ach.* 676-718 (n.b.716); *Knights* 1373-81; *Wasps* 686-90; cf. the agon of *Clouds*.

The ultimate fall-back of the comic dramatist wishing to satirise rich aristocrats is the cliché neatly summed up in *Frogs* 739-40; 'of course my master is a gentleman', says Xanthias, ὅστις γε πίνειν οἶδε καὶ βινεῖν μόνον.[68] One fragment of Eupolis (fr. 208=221) fits Cimon into this cliché, and gives it a neat twist: 'he wasn't a *bad* man, but over-fond of the drink, and rather neglectful; sometimes he used to sleep in Sparta, leaving Elpinice here all alone'; this is a barbed reference to Cimon's alleged incest with his sister.[69] A person unnamed is satirised for extravagance in both fields and for inventiveness in the former in Eupolis fr. 351=385; the passage is obscure, but Meineke's conjecture that Alcibiades is meant may well be right.[70] Alcibiades appears surprisingly infrequently in Aristophanes and the fragments of other dramatists. De Ste Croix believes that this may be politically signifi-cant;[71] it may be (though we have so far found little trace of political *Tendenz* in Aristophanes' choice of comic target), but equally it may be due to the loss of relevant evidence. We know, for example, from testimonia that Alcibiades was the butt of Eupolis' *Baptae*, but one would not have guessed it from the surviving fragments of the play. The guess that Aristophanes' *Triphales* gave Alcibiades the title role is not supported by any real evidence;[72] but it has its attractions (Alcibiades' reputation would make him uniquely suited to the part), and the impossibility of knowing anything certain about this play, as about so many others, should remind us of the need for caution in interpreting apparent silences.[73]

---

[68] 'Soaking and poking' is David Barrett's felicitous rendering of the assonance (*The Wasps etc.* [Harmondsworth 1964] 84); for 'soaking' see also *Wasps* 79-80 (MacDowell's note *ad loc.* is misconceived: that the terms can be applied to slaves does not mean that they can have no social connotation here, and the joke is enfeebled if they do not; for the ironical use of χρηστός see also *Wealth* 155-6, cited above).

[69] It should deter us from reading Eupolis' political views out of frr.117=384, 205=219, with their praise of the 'godlike' leaders of old; Aristophanes was evidently not the only comic poet to use the 'good old days' motif opportunistically.

[70] He cites Pliny *NH* 14.143-5 for 351.3; and the identification gives point to the (admittedly lacunose) first couplet. (Meineke's conjecture is to be found in the *Supplementa addendorum*, vol. 5 p. lxxxvi.)

[71] De Ste Croix (n.6) 361-2.

[72] Only fr. 554 connects the play with Alcibiades, and that is reassigned to *Banqueters* by Kassel-Austin (fr. 244).

[73] References to Alcibiades (apart from *Frogs* 1422-34) are to his affectations (*Ach.* 716, *Wasps* 44-6, fr. 198=205, cf. Archippus fr. 45), and to his homo- and heterosexual excesses: fr. 554=244 (see previous note; it is relevant, whatever its source), fr. 907KA, Pherecrates fr. 155 (cf. D.L.4.49), Eupolis fr.158=171, fr.adesp.3. (One should not forget in this connection that Alcibiades' private life was a public

It might be objected that these satirical thrusts at the rich and at individual rich victims are not directed against the rich 'as such'.[74] It is true that Aristophanes does not laugh at people simply because they have money; he laughs at them because they have money and vices, or money and affectations. Since the affectations are restricted to the rich, and the vices are sometimes alleged to be universal among the rich, this might be thought a distinction without a great deal of difference. Nevertheless it should be stressed that we should not expect Aristophanes to satirise the rich *as such*, any more that he does the handsome, the brave or the talented *as such*. In Aristophanes above all, the laughable is what is odd, grotesque or deformed;[75] there is nothing odd, grotesque or deformed, and therefore nothing laughable, about having wealth and so forth *as such*: they are qualities one admires and envies in those who possess them. Hence the inevitable recourse in satirising such people (and one will want to satirise them, since one admires *and envies*) is to point to or invent concomitant attributes and attack these; this is what Aristophanes does.

We found in *Wealth* that the poor disapproved of the rich, and that they wanted to become rich themselves. There is no real contradiction here; everyone is inclined to believe that he or she would behave

---

and political issue: Th.6.15.3–4, 28.2, Plut.*Alc*.16.) De Ste Croix also claims (p. 362) that the comic poets' gentle treatment of Nicias is politically significant; the same cautions are necessary, and note also that he understates the satirical thrust of the references: in them Nicias appears as timid (Phrynichus fr.59, contrasting him with a πολίτης ἀγαθός) and dilatory (*Birds* 640), while Aristophanes fr.100=102 is fairly clearly a jibe at his ceding the Pylos command to Cleon (in spite of de Ste Croix's enigmatic doubts); these were politically damaging charges outside the theatre: Th.6.18.6–7 (cf. Gomme, *JHS* 71 [1951] 79), Plut.*Nic*.8. Telecleides fr.41 implies that Nicias has some (unspecified) guilty secret; in Eupolis fr.181=193 he is described by Plutarch as κωμῳδούμενος: de Ste Croix says that the fragment is 'warmly appreciative', but without access to the context we are in no position to reject Plutarch's assessment. (Nicias' appearance in Eupolis' *Demes*, fr.91=105, is due to an implausible conjecture in the text of Galen, and should be discounted; see K. Plepelits, *Die Fragmente der Demen des Eupolis* [Vienna 1970] 28.)

[74] Cf. de Ste Croix (n.6) 360: 'Aristophanes scarcely says a disrespectful word about the rich as such . . . the rich are never once attacked as such'; Sommerstein, in his commentary on *Ach.*, adds that 'the poor quite often are satirised as such' (p. 25 n. 28). Dover (n.22) 45 n.24 is rightly sceptical of the significance of this.

[75] One should not underestimate the element of ἐπιχαιρεκακία in Aristophanes: the Megarian in *Ach.* is a good instance (MacDowell [n.27] 156–8 finds sympathy here, but I am unable to detect it); see also fr. 64=71 ('a joke in rather bad taste, at the expense of . . . the Samians', Forrest [n.27] 19–20) and *Birds* 186 ('Melian hunger'); at *Peace* 478–80, despite the eirenic context, Aristophanes cannot resist a jibe at the Spartan prisoners from Pylos (nor against the Megarians: 481–3, 500–2).

much better if enriched than those who are now rich do (this is precisely what Chremylus claims of himself in 245 ff., doubtless with better reason than most of us). But we have now added admiration to the mix of attitudes, and this does give rise to a certain inconsistency; for one may desire wealth *per se*, but to *admire* wealth implies that one believes it to consort with other and admirable traits. I do not think, however, that this inconsistency reflects a flaw in the analysis; rather, the ambivalent attitude to the rich is one which may plausibly be attributed to Athenian πένητες, in whose culture wealth and aristocratic breeding retained (and would continue to retain) significant prestige and influence, although ultimate political power had long been vested with the *demos*. Hence when Aristophanes incorporates an admiring attitude towards the wealthy and well-born into his mockery of contemporary politics this is not to be understood as the expression of a distinctively upper-class and 'paternalist' bias;[76] rather he is for satirical purposes pushing to its extreme one of the tendencies in the complex social attitude of the Athenian *demos*, just as he elsewhere pushes the opposite tendency to its extreme, again for satirical purposes.

We may use as an illustrative case Aristophanes' treatment of Cleon. We can confidently assert that Cleon was a very wealthy man: leisure, and therefore wealth, were preconditions of political activity at the highest levels; there is evidence that Cleon's father performed an expensive liturgy in 460/59; and one may recall that Aristophanes could envisage Cleon and his circle at a high-class dinner party (*Wasps* 1220-1).[77] The 'handle' of the joke against Cleon is that he did not belong to one of the established leading families, and that his wealth (though inherited) was ultimately derived from industrial slave-owning rather than the traditionally respectable landed sources. By a familiar process of comic distortion these, perhaps distant, disreputable connections are wildly exaggerated and projected onto Cleon's person; the result is the vulgar tanner familiar from *Knights* and elsewhere. Two points must be made. First we must qualify an observation made in (8). We remarked there that abuse of individuals

---

[76] De Ste Croix (n.6) 357–62, 374–6; contrast Dover (n.22) 34–45, with whose cautiously expressed conclusion I agree. (Relevant passages are *Knights* 128–45, 177–94, 738–40, *Frogs* 718–37; cf. also Eupolis frr.117=384, 205=219, with n.69 above.)

[77] See MacDowell *ad loc.*; for the first two points see de Ste Croix (n.6) 235 n.7, and J. K. Davies, *Wealth and the Power of Wealth in Classical Athens* (New York 1981).

was not committed to veracity in oratory or in comedy; but whereas the orator may be indifferent to falsehood so long as he can make his opponent lose face, the comedian is likely to have a positive interest in falsehood, since a perceived discrepancy between caricature and reality is a rich source of amusement. Aristophanes' portrayal of Cleon is funny partly because it is, and is meant to be recognised as, fantasy.[78] Thus most of Aristophanes' audience would not outside the theatre have granted the antecedent of the inference, crucial to Aristophanes' joke against Cleon, 'Cleon is a vulgar tanner, therefore he is unfit to exercise political leadership'; but (and this is the second point) having granted the antecedent in the fantasising context of a comedy they would probably not have resisted or resented the inference to the consequent. The reaction of Aristophanes' sausage-seller may be cited here. Although he enters into the fray enthusiastically once he has been convinced that his social disadvantages ideally qualify him for a political career, his initial reaction is one of incredulity: 'I am only a sausage-seller, low-born and uneducated; how can I become an ἀνήρ, an important and influential person?' (*Knights* 178–9).[79] We must allow for humour in this passage, but the humour comes from the counter-argument that these qualities are in fact essential to the politically ambitious, and the sausage-seller's initially sceptical reaction is (allowing that the situation as a whole is grotesquely unlikely) verisimilar. We must distinguish between the exercise of political leadership and the right of access to political debate and participation in political decision-making. The latter right was jealously guarded by the ordinary Athenian, and it is in this sense that ultimate political control was vested with the *demos*; as a matter of practical necessity political leadership remained with the wealthier classes, and this practical necessity was reinforced by, and in turn reinforced, the prestige of wealth and (to a lesser extent) of aristocratic descent.

---

[78] A curious illustration of the failure to grasp the fantasising nature of Aristophanes' comedy can be found in MacDowell (n.27) 147, on the ambassadors in *Ach..* He recognises two questions: (a) would Aristophanes have approved of ambassadors acting in the way these ambassadors act, and (b) did Athenian ambassadors 'as a matter of historical fact' act in this way? But one must also ask (c) did Aristophanes think, or expect his audience to think, that Athenian ambassadors acted in this way in reality? If the answer to (c) is negative (as seems plausible), then one cannot without further argument infer from a positive answer to (a) to an intent to excite disapproval of the real ambassadors.

[79] The implication, perhaps unintended, in Dover (n. 22) 44 that the sausage-seller 'proclaims' his poor birth 'with pride' is incorrect; it is his instructor who values poor birth, while the sausage-seller still sees it as a reason for shame and as a disqualification from politics.

If we accept this line of argument it will enable us to avoid a paradoxical consequence of de Ste Croix's reading of Aristophanes. The paradox is particularly evident in a passage such as this:

It would only be among the snobs like Aristophanes that one would then 'lose face' because one's fortune (or, more likely, that of one's father or grandfather ...) originally came from industry or trade. Not a few of those among Aristophanes' audience who laughed at his nasty little jokes about the 'demagogues' he so detested must have been tradesmen of one sort or another and are not likely to have felt demeaned by their calling.[80]

But if the 'tradesmen' among Aristophanes' audience found his 'nasty little jokes' funny, as de Ste Croix admits that they did ('who *laughed* at his ... jokes'), then the social outlook which those jokes presuppose is one which they shared with him; if so, then we cannot infer from the jokes that their author was a 'snob', or indeed that he 'detested' the demagogues (any more than did his audience, who laughed at the jokes and voted for their victims). De Ste Croix observes elsewhere that the orators' use of social terminology 'might ... be dictated by considerations of prudence' since 'an orator's audience in the Assembly or the courts would naturally contain a good number of poor men';[81] but precisely the same is true of the comic dramatist's audience,[82] and one would not have expected a comic dramatist to have achieved before such an audience the acclaim that Aristophanes achieved if he were articulating views distinctive of a very restricted section of Athenian society, as de Ste Croix's analysis would imply. That difficult conclusion is, I have argued, unnecessary.

## 10. The Power of the Demos

The paradox we have detected in de Ste Croix's treatment of Aristophanic attitudes to class and social structure arises elsewhere in his analysis. Commenting on Aristophanes' caricature of the Athenian

---

[80] De Ste Croix, *The Class Struggle in the Ancient Greek World* (London 1981) 125.

[81] De Ste Croix (n.6) 376; but Dover (n.22) 30–7 remarks on the *similarities* between social attitudes in oratory and comedy.

[82] On the comic audience see (3) above; it should be emphasised again that 'poor' means 'not rich', and that a graph showing the distribution of wealth in classical Athens would be steeply inclined at its upper end: see Davies (n.77) 34–7.

courts, and in particular on his frequent and disrespectful references to jury-pay, de Ste Croix remarks that this was 'in itself not in the least funny, except of course to a member of the upper classes, who disapproved of it to the extent of thinking it a fit subject for satire'; again: 'very little of this is at all funny, except to someone who sees the whole system as a form of popular tyranny, and is out to discredit by ridicule'.[83] But de Ste Croix himself lays it down as an axiom that the comedian 'must always be *funny*';[84] and this must mean funny to his audience. Either Aristophanes violated this axiom (but why, then, did he persist when he found that his jokes were being received in stony silence?); or else (and his success as a comic poet points to this alternative) his audience did find these jokes funny. But then the joke was more widely available than de Ste Croix allows, and we can no longer use it as evidence for Aristophanes' distinctively upper-class outlook. The conclusion that satire of the jury system was widely popular in Athens is not an easy one to resist, since we have no independent evidence of who did or did not find it funny; de Ste Croix's view is speculative, and is very unconvincing, resting as it seems to do on the premise that one can only see as 'a fit subject for satire' that of which one disapproves.

Residual doubts may be laid to rest if we now remark de Ste Croix's misrepresentation of Aristophanes' satire on the courts. We are told that the poet 'clearly resented the power the *demos* was beginning to exercise, more particularly in the law courts, as a result of dicastic pay', and that his caricature of the courts is 'a very clever attack upon the system which enabled many humble men, gulled (as Aristophanes would have us believe) by "the demagogues", to sit in judgement on their betters'.[85] But is it the political power exercised by humble men at the expense of the upper classes that affronts Bdelycleon? He complains that they have *no* power, that the power of which his father boasts is an 'unwashed arse' (*Wasps* 604). It is the power exercised by politicians at the expense of humble men that infuriates him. He does indeed think that the masses are being gulled by their political leaders, who keep them content on a pittance while pocketing for themselves nine-tenths of the city's revenue *and* huge allied bribes (664–79, 682–95). But the thing that he finds objectionable in this is that the

---

[83] De Ste Croix (n.6) 362; cf. 357: 'his frequent sneers at [dicastic pay] betray the irritation felt by the upper-class Athenian at this innovation of the radical democracy'.

[84] De Ste Croix (n.6) 357.

[85] De Ste Croix (n.6) 362 n.9.

money wasted on self-seeking politicians could be used to keep decent, ordinary people in the lap of luxury (698–712); and this he thinks the right of the Athenian *demos*, earned by its military exertions – by land, be it noted, *and by sea* (684–5, 711): there is no social restrictiveness here.[86] Similarly in the parabasis the Chorus argue for restricted eligibility for dicastic pay; but the restriction they urge is to those who have seen active service by land or sea (1102–21, cf. 1075–1101).[87]

In *Wasps* and elsewhere (in the satire on profiteers in *Acharnians*, for example, or on Cleon in *Knights*, especially 801–9, 1207–28), Aristophanes' line is not upper-class at all, but popular; it is the interests of the *demos* and of the ordinary man that he wants to see served.[88] Since the passages cited are (of course) jocular (no Athenian citizen could really have believed that the city's revenue might be devoted wholly to providing subsidised bird's milk for every citizen), this conclusion is consistent with the supposition of a devious strategy on Aristophanes' part; on this view he would be using populist comedy rather cynically to discredit the system to anti-populist ends, toadying to and deceiving the *demos* like the politicians of his fantasy. But there is nothing at all to suggest that this supposition would be correct. That is not to say that we can simply identify the political and social assumptions of the plays with Aristophanes' extratheatrical political convictions. If my analysis is correct, the plays are so nicely attuned to the prejudices and expectations of the majority of Aristophanes' audience that one would hesitate to affirm of anything in them that it was put there in order to express Aristophanes' own

---

[86] Thus while we may agree with de Ste Croix that Aristophanes thought that 'the tribute should be used in the interests of "nicer" people' ([n.6] 368, quoting Forrest [n.28] 1 n.3), we must add that for Aristophanes the 'nicer' people are those who have served the people well – πολῖται χρηστοί in the sense of *Ach.* 595, men who have been ἄνδρες ἀγαθοὶ περὶ τὴν πόλιν (*Ach.* 697) – and the people than whom they are 'nicer' are politicians.

[87] In *Knights* 565–8 the same polar expression shows that the Chorus is praising the forebears of *all* Athenians; in 576 ff. they offer their own contribution to the public good, contrasting themselves with the self-seeking generals of 573–6.

[88] A final example of this kind of misrepresentation in de Ste Croix: 'of course Aristophanes is particularly hostile to those who brought prosecutions ("sycophants") ... It was naturally the propertied class, to which Aristophanes himself belonged and with which he sympathised, which had most to fear from "sycophants"' ([n.6] 362–3 n.10). The latter sentence may be true 'as a matter of historical fact'; but a quick census of those victimised by and objecting to sycophants in the passages which de Ste Croix there cites will show that it is not from the point of view of the propertied class that Aristophanes presents the matter.

political views; on this point, agnosticism is in order. But for the purposes of the plays Aristophanes' 'views', the postures he adopts, are as I have described them. Poverty, tutelar deity of the ordinary man, will provide a summary (and on this point, at least, Chremylus concurs: *Wealth* 567–71): the men to be praised (the πολῖται χρηστοί) are those who, even if they are poor, speak and act in the interests of the *demos* and the city; the villains are those who, enriching themselves at public expense, turn against the masses and make war upon the *demos*.

## 11. Conclusion

Let us now sum up briefly the conclusions that have been reached. In our discussion of *Clouds* (2) we found external evidence suggesting that apparently bitter satirical abuse in comedy was compatible with the absence of hostile intent on the part of the poet; external evidence, in particular the case of *Knights* (3), indicated that the audience's enjoyment of comic abuse was similarly compatible with a favourable attitude to the victim outside the theatre. The political and military context of *Lysistrata* (4) deterred us from seeing peace as it appears in that play as a seriously intended programme in real politics; consequently the devices which render Lysistrata's speech in favour of peace comic could be accepted as a substitute for, rather than as a vehicle of, serious intent. An analogous view was taken of the comic devices surrounding Dicaeopolis' speech in favour of peace in *Acharnians* (5), once arguments purporting to establish serious intent had been answered. The apparent inconsistency of this with Aristophanes' claims to the role of adviser disappeared when it was realised that this claim is itself usually treated light-heartedly in comedy (6); similarly the abuse of the audience (7) and of individuals (8) proved to have been disarmed by incorporation into a purely comic and fantastic realm. We then found (9) that the application of terms such as χρηστός and καλὸς κἀγαθός in Aristophanes was primarily moral and patriotic; wealth was not a criterion (on the contrary, the wealthy were sometimes seen in a decidedly hostile light), except where the prestige of wealth was being exploited to satirise contemporary politics. The range of social attitudes displayed in the plays was shown to be characteristic of the modestly prosperous strata of society from which many of Aristophanes' heroes and probably the majority of his audience were drawn; consistent with the popular bias was the conclu-

sion that Aristophanes writes from the standpoint of a defender of
the power and interests of the *demos,* of the mass of ordinary citizens
against their exploitative leaders (10).

It will be clear from this summary that Aristophanic comedy is and
is not, in my view, political. It is political, in the sense that contemporary political life is its point of departure; political reality is taken up by
the poet and subjected to the ignominious transformations of comic
fantasy. But the product of the fantasising process did not and was not
intended to have a reciprocal effect on political reality; comedy had
no designs on the political life from which it departed, and in that
sense was not political. Politics was the material of comedy, but
comedy did not in turn aspire to be a political force. This is a reading
which some might decry as 'aestheticist'; but that would be a mistake.
The view that literature in general or comedy in particular cannot or
ought not to aspire to political effect has not been a premise of my
argument (as it appears to have been in Gomme's, for example); it is in
fact a view that I would reject. Rather, I have tried to set the plays in a
particular context and to make sense of the resulting corpus of historical data; right or wrong, it purports to be a historically rooted reading.

Consequently it is capable of throwing light on the context in turn;
if my interpretation is correct, it will contribute something to our
understanding of the way in which the *demos* maintained and exercised its political control in late fifth-century Athens, disarming the
potentially critical platform that certain traditional concepts of the
poet's role might have made available to the comic dramatist.[89] This is
certainly the view taken by the pseudo-Xenophontine oligarch (*Ath.
Pol.*2.18). He oversimplifies somewhat when he claims that the *demos*
is not κωμῳδούμενος; it is, regularly. But that, as we have seen, is part of
an amiable and bantering intimacy between poet and audience; individual victims are, as the oligarch claims, in general rich, well-born or
powerful.[90] On the available evidence, the oligarch possessed neither

---

[89] Similarly in the case of tragedy: it will be noted that the political positions
detected in Euripides by de Ste Croix ([n.6] 356–7 n.1) are all patriotic and democratic in tendency, reflecting the same ideology of the μέσοι that we found in
Aristophanes; and I believe that the *Oresteia* should also be read as a patriotic and
pan-Athenian play, consensual rather than partisan (see the discussion in my
*Poetics of Greek Tragedy* [London 1987] 64–71). The reaction to Phrynichus' *Sack
of Miletus* (Hdt.6.21.1–2) may be the earliest evidence for the exercise of this kind
of control by the *demos.*

[90] The terms used here he often restricts to right-minded oligarchs like himself;
but no one who had seen a comedy could have intended that restriction here,
excluding democratic leaders, and it need not be so read. (Note Aristophanes'
boast that he attacks οἱ μέγιστοι: *Clouds* 549, *Wasps* 1030, *Peace* 751.)

the most attractive personality nor the most penetrating intellect of Athenians of his time; but he did have some insights into the workings of Athenian democracy, and on the control of the theatre by the *demos* he was right. Aristophanes told his audience what they wanted to hear; they rewarded him for it.

## *Appendix: Unity in Aristophanic Comedy*

In (6) we observed that the apparently serious intent of the parabasis of *Frogs* could not be discerned also in the action of that play. It is true that the rival poets are tested on their ability to give political advice, and that the advice which Aristophanes gave in the parabasis is repeated; but it is repeated by the poet who loses the contest, the result of which does not seem to reflect an evaluation of the advice offered that could be taken seriously outside the theatre. In short, the play's serious parabasis digresses from the comic fantasy in which it is embedded. A similar discrepancy was observed in *Acharnians*; here the credit which Aristophanes claims in the parabasis for his services to the Athenian *demos* is inconsistent with the premises of the satire of the *demos* in the preceding action, while the jocularly 'hawkish' stance he adopts in the parabasis is opposed to the (in my view, no less jocular) advocacy of peace in the play's action. Other instances were cited from *Knights, Clouds* and *Birds* (n.37) – and the survey was by no means exhaustive. The obvious conclusion is that Aristophanes adopts positions opportunistically; his comic purposes in any given play are not necessarily consistent with each other, and even when – as in the parabasis of *Frogs* – he has a 'serious' intent, he does not pursue that intent outside a limited and clearly marked context.

If we are to think of an Aristophanic comedy as unified, therefore, it cannot be as the consistent exposition of some single theme or intention. But that is precisely the dominant approach to unity in recent criticism of Old Comedy, as of other Greek poetic genres.[91] Does it

---

[91] E.g., T. Gelzer, *RE Suppl.* XII(1970)1543: 'Die Einheit der Komödien des Aristophanes ist, soweit sie überhaupt durchgeführt ist, bestimmt vom Thema her, das in jedem Stück im Sinne des χρηστὰ τῇ πόλει λέγειν behandelt wird ... Das Thema bildet jeweils ein außerhalb des Stücks selber liegendes Problem aus der Wirklichkeit in Athen. Personen, Handlung, phantastische und realistische Darstellungsmittel, dramatische und undramatische Teile sind nicht um ihrer selbst

follow that an Aristophanic play is just 'eine lose Abfolge von Kabarettnummern'?[92] In this appendix I shall argue that this is not the case,
and that the unifying element in Aristophanic comedy is – perhaps
surprisingly – plot.[93]

Let us take *Frogs* as a first example. There are a number of objec-
tions which must be faced if we are to regard the plot of *Frogs* as
providing the play with a coherent unifying structure. Like many
Aristophanic comedies, the play falls into two parts around the parabasis. The first of these parts is a loose series of miscellaneous incidents lacking (it is sometimes alleged) the interconnection one expects
of a well-ordered plot; the second part introduces the contest between
the poets, a motif wholly unrelated to the quest-plot which the first
part initiates; and when the quest-motif is reintroduced towards the
end of the second part, it is presented in a light wholly inconsistent

willen konzipiert, sondern zur Darstellung gewisser Aspekte und zur besonderen
Charakterisierung dieses Themas ... Darauf beziehen sich die Witze, dafür werden
gewisse Symbole und Bilder erfunden, die durch das ganze Stück hindurch immer
wieder den Bezug auf das Thema herstellen.' (Gelzer cites K. D. Koch, *Kritische
Idee und komisches Thema* [Bremen 1965].) A somewhat different version of the
same general approach is found in K. McLeish, *The Theatre of Aristophanes*
(London 1980) 64, 66: 'Unless what he sees is to seem merely chaotic, the spectator
of a play must be aware ... of some sort of unifiying structure ... Usually this
structure is bound up with the main philosophical theme of the play, and the events
of the plot serve as a particular demonstration of that theme applied to human
affairs ... Underlying all the hilarious incident of each plot is a unifying philosophical idea, as didactic as that of tragedy ...' I have argued against this approach to
unity in tragedy in the work already cited (n.89), and will be developing the theme
in relation to other genres elsewhere.
[92] E. R. Schwinge, *Maia* 27(1975)199, argues that 'die aristophanische Komödie
ja nie eine lose Abfolge von Kabarettnummern ist; sie ist stets insofern von
bestimmter Kohärenz, als jedes Stück, und zwar als Ganzes, von *einem* komischen
Einfall gibt ... Aber der komische Einfall ist nie etwas Autonomes ... Aristophanes
verfolgt mit dem komischen Einfall stets eine bestimmte politische Wirkungs-
absicht; das komische Thema ... verdankt sich immer einer kritischen Idee'
(Schwinge, like Gelzer, is indebted to Koch); the implied 'either/or' is revealing.
[93] 'The loose plot-structure of Athenian Old Comedy has often baffled, per-
plexed and irritated historians of Greek literature. Measured against an Aristotelian ideal of unified plot, the unfortunate comic dramatist is pictured as struggling
in the darkness with only limited success towards the light of Menandrian
perfection': J. Vaio, *GRBS* 14(1973)369; cf. A. O. Hulton, *G&R* 19(1972)35: 'Or-
ganic unity ... was more the prerogative of Greek tragedy than Aristophanic
Comedy'. The contrast between comedy and tragedy is developed at length and (in
my view) misleadingly by M. Landfester, *Handlungsverlauf und Komik in den
frühen Komödien des Aristophanes* (Berlin & New York 1977) 1–15; as for Aristotle, we shall return to him later.

with its original form. How can such a ramshackle structure be taken seriously as a unifying factor? Are we not compelled to look for some thematic integration of its dislocated parts – or else to accept that the play is indeed only a loose string of centrifugal jokes?

We may begin by examining the play's chief inconsistency. Dionysus' initial intention is to bring Euripides back from Hades: his desire is quite specific as to the poet in question (52–4, 66–7); towards the end of the play, however (1418–9), Dionysus claims that his intention was to bring back a poet – no individual is specified – and adds that his aim in so doing was the salvation of Athens (and so the perpetuation of his own annual celebration). This additional element is not only unmentioned in the original specific statement of intent; Dionysus there positively suggests otherwise: for example, the recovery of Euripides is seen as a rascally escapade (80–1), a view of the enterprise far removed from the elevated tone of patriotic service which subsequently emerges. There are sound comic reasons why Dionysus' initial desire must be for Euripides; Euripides, not Aeschylus or even Sophocles, is a stock joke on the Aristophanic stage, and the poet cannot afford to pass over the opportunity, not only to write jokes about Euripides into his opening scene, but also to put his audience into a receptive mood by engaging all the expectations they had acquired about Euripides in comedy. Moreover, the initial intention to recover Euripides sets up the splendid joke in 1469–71, where Dionysus turns back on Euripides his own morally dubious sophistry about oaths;[94] Aristophanes' careful preparation for this joke, and the clear reference back to Dionysus' original intention when the trap is sprung, strongly suggest that the inconsistency is calculated, rather than casual. If Dionysus' initial intent must be to retrieve Euripides, it is equally desirable that this intent should be suppressed during the agon; Dionysus is invited to adjudicate as an expert in the field (810–11), and if he were still seen as a partisan of Euripides, this partiality would interfere with his role. It is for this reason that the enthusiast for trendy Euripidean λαλία (89–107) has by 916–7 acquired more conservative sympathies – another inconsequentiality in the plot. But if the original intention of Dionysus' quest must be suppressed in the second part of the play, the quest-motif itself cannot

---

[94] Dionysus has not sworn an oath; but he starts with the firm intention of bringing Euripides back, and it is to this that Euripides appeals with an understandable (if, in the circumstances, ill-advised) exaggeration. Note that the inconsistency concerning Dionysus' intention is not just between the beginning and end of the play, but is built into this single scene (1418–9 *vs* 1469–71).

be wholly abandoned: for one thing, the successful achievement of a goal makes an effective climax to a play; more importantly, the motif has been too important in the first part of the play for it to be left unresolved – precisely because Aristophanes *is* concerned to secure continuity and completeness for his plot. Thus the quest has to be retained, but a new goal must be substituted: hence 1418-9. The intention of saving the city, which would have been quite out of keeping with the tone of the opening scene, obviously fits very well at the end of the agon, in which the didactic responsibility of the poet has been emphasised. And the infiltration of this new idea is eased by the existence in comedy of a typical plot, in which the city in direst extremity is saved by some ingenious device – such as the recovery of a dead poet (Eupolis' *Demes* is an apposite parallel: cf. (7) above); the familiarity of this plot-type would tend to distract the audience from the inconsistency which the insertion of its fundamental topos into *Frogs* produces.

The inconsistencies in *Frogs* do not show, therefore, that Aristophanes was not concerned to produce a coherent plot. On the contrary, he has cleverly ensured the continuity and completion of the quest-plot, while manipulating its elements as unobtrusively as possible so as to maximise its comic effect at each point. This, so far from being a distinctively comic device, is a technique familiar from tragedy. An obvious example is Sophocles' *Oedipus Tyrannos*, the plot of which is (rightly) much admired, but which depends on a whole web of concealed implausibilities and inconsistencies.[95] For example, Oedipus' failure to grasp the significance of Teiresias' accusations would be hard to accept if he were thought of at that stage of the play as possessing the knowledge which is later attributed to him – that his parentage had been questioned, and that Apollo's oracle had foretold his parricide and incest (*OT* 774-93); when Teiresias is on stage, however, the audience, having not yet been told any of this, is in no position to regard Oedipus in that light; they are therefore less likely to find his reaction implausible. In effect, Oedipus does not know in the earlier scenes of the play what he later has known all along; but this is an unobtrusive inconsistency. Oedipus' changing states of knowledge are analogous to Dionysus' retrospectively redefined intentions. The comic poet may take greater liberties than the tragedian – his genre is, after all, more relaxed; but the liberties which he takes

---

[95] See, for example, D. Bain, *G&R* 26(1979)132-45, and pp. 6-23 of Dawe's edition of the play; I have discussed the topic briefly in the section on dramatic conviction in the book previously cited (n.89).

differ in degree, not in kind, from those of tragedy, and in neither genre is a libertine handling of plot incompatible with its unifying function.

How is the quest-plot treated in the first part of *Frogs?* It is true that the individual incidents do not follow one from another in necessary or probable sequence; the order in which the inhabitants of Hades appear once the travellers have arrived outside Pluto's palace, for example, is determined not causally, but by the requirements of the joke as Dionysus and his slave change places. Nevertheless, it is necessary or probable (once one has granted the fantastic premises of the plot, naturally) that incidents of this kind should occur on a journey to Hades; the travellers have these experiences not merely on the way to Hades, but *because* they are on the way to Hades. Indeed, the incidents all help or hinder their progress: the travellers seek advice from a previous visitor to the Underworld, cross (or circumambulate) the bottomless lake, are deterred by (perhaps imaginary) dangers, seek directions from the locals, and encounter various difficulties in gaining entry to Pluto's palace. Given a plot based on a quest or journey, then whatever events help towards or obstruct the attaining of the goal are causally integral to the plot; and in this case the much-delayed entry into the palace visibly enacts the travellers' arrival.[96] This is their first goal; but they have come here for a purpose, and the business yet to be transacted – the recovery of Euripides – must retain the audience's interest and carry their expectations across the interruption of the action in the parabasis.

Yet this unfinished business is not taken up after the parabasis. Instead, the matter of the contest between Aeschylus and Euripides is introduced. Again, this development cannot be regarded as a necessary or probable consequence of Dionysus' quest or of his arrival; nevertheless, the synchronicity of his arrival with the contest is not merely coincidental. The contest has come about because Euripides has died; and Euripides' death is what prompted Dionysus' journey;[97]

---

[96] Cf. E. Fraenkel, *Beobachtungen zu Aristophanes* (Rome 1962) 180–1: 'Hingegen finden wir in dem der Parabase vorangehenden Teil der Frösche zwar auch eine Reihe von Einzelszenen..., aber durch alle diese Einzelszenen läuft eine continuierliche Handlung, bis schließlich Dionysos, am Ziel seiner schwierigen Reise angelangt, mit seinem Diener in das Haus des Pluton eintritt.'

[97] Sophocles' death is presented as a *sine qua non* of Dionysus' desire (since it deprives him of the consolation of a good poet surviving), rather than as a cause. Whether or not his death supervened on a plot already conceived, Sophocles had to be elided, since he would obscure the old/new opposition on which the contest

it is therefore hardly surprising that he arrives in Hades just when the contest is in prospect. The quest and the contest are related as necessary or probable consequences of a single cause;[98] and in 1416 ff., Pluto's attempt to force his arbitrator off the fence cleverly links the two motifs: the result of the contest will supply Dionysus with the goal of his quest. Viewed in this light the plot of *Frogs* seems consequent and well-ordered, well able to bear the weight of unification.

Another play in which the action is interrupted by the parabasis is *Wasps*. The two parts of this play are, considered thematically, only tenuously related: the first part is devoted to a political satire centred on the courts, while in the second part the comedy derives from the attempt to insert Philocleon into elegant society. This thematic divergence has, inevitably, caused concern to recent interpreters;[99] yet the causal integration of these thematically divergent elements could scarcely be improved upon. Bdelycleon's first problem is to curb his father's obsessive passion for jury service: he begins by confining him forcibly to the house, and in 514–21 manages to manoeuvre Philocleon into submitting the evaluation of his chosen way of life to arbitration – an advance, since Bdelycleon, being clever and right, is bound to win any rational debate. Bdelycleon's arguments are designed to show that the members of the *public* jury panels are being exploited by their political masters; it is therefore natural that he should try to temper the disillusioned Philocleon's despair by indulging his obsession with an innocuous *private* trial (750–66). But this is a trick: bemused by his son's tear-jerking rhetoric in defence of the dog Labes, Philocleon allows himself to be steered towards the wrong voting-urn; the shock of this acquittal finally breaks his dicastic morale. Philocleon's collapse immediately precedes the parabasis; what continuation is more natural after this interruption than that Bdelycleon should set about rebuilding his father's shattered life – and that he should find the old man somewhat less tractable material than he had hoped? In fact, this reconstruction of Philocleon's way of

---

between Aeschylus and Euripides is based (see K. J. Dover [n.37] 180–1); and this has been done with elegant compliments.

[98] Thus it is not true to say (e.g.) that 'Drexlers Thronosmotiv . . . von außen und zufällig auf die Achse der Handlung trifft' (F. Richter, quoted by H. Erbse, *Gnomon* 28[1956]273); still less that 'the presence of Dionysus alone . . . unites the two parts of the play' (C. P. Segal, *HSCP* 65 [1961] 208).

[99] E.g., T. Long, *ICS* 1 (1976) 15: 'The great difficulty in defending the quality of the play is the relationship of the first part, with its theme of "juryitis", to the second with its attempts to reeducate Philocleon.'

life has been Bdelycleon's declared intention throughout (341, 503–6, 719–24); a reaffirmation of this plan is strategically placed before the parabasis (1003–6) to reinforce our expectations of the story's post-parabatic development. Not only, therefore, does the plot of *Wasps* possess an admirable causal continuity, but the dramatist has taken care to emphasise that continuity by the use of proleptic allusions.[100] To defend the unity of the play, it is not necessary to go beyond this causal structure in an attempt to establish some elusive thematic integration.[101]

Aristophanes' desire to underline the continuity of his plot is evident also in *Thesmophoriazusae*. Euripides' initial problem in this play is to infiltrate a sympathiser into the women's assembly – a persuasive speaker (184–7), who could pass himself off as a woman (190–2): Agathon is the obvious choice. When Agathon declines the commission,[102] Euripides' relative volunteers to go; he lacks all the necessary qualifications, but in a crisis one cannot pick and choose, and with Agathon's assistance something can be done to make him look less blatantly incongruous. Nevertheless, the unsuitability of Euripides' agent makes a miscarriage likely (as it turns out, his inability to make a tactful and persuasive speech brings him to the verge of discovery in 566–70, even before Cleisthenes' arrival seals his fate); and the relative prudently ensures that Euripides is committed to his rescue if anything should go wrong (269–76) – a clear pointer to the subsequent development of the plot. This pointer is reactivated in 765 ff., when the relative sends out his appeal for assistance; this immediately precedes the parabasis, and the allusion to Euripides' *Palamedes* is elegantly used to construct a bridge across the interruption: when the parabasis is over, the relative realises his mistake in choosing a play as bad as *Palamedes* – Euripides must be too ashamed to show his face (847–8). By choosing a play with a female principal, he can at least turn his disguise to advantage (850–1); this introduces the burlesques

---

[100] Rightly emphasised by D. M. MacDowell, *Aristophanes: Wasps* (Oxford 1971) 6–7.

[101] See, for example, Long (n.99); J. Vaio, *GRBS* 12 (1971) 335–51.

[102] As a passive homosexual, Agathon is in sexual competition with the women, who are therefore even more hostile to him than to Euripides (203–9). Dover, *Greek Homosexuality* (London 1978) 141, surely misunderstands Agathon's excuse; μὲν οὖν accepts Agathon's point, while substituting a stronger term – see Denniston, *Greek Particles*² (Oxford 1954) 475. (Note that Cleisthenes, on much the same evidence, is treated as the women's sympathiser and proxenos [574–6]: a small example of Aristophanes' opportunism.)

of *Helen* and *Andromeda* to which the latter part of the play is devoted.[103]

Rau remarks on 'die Verschiebung der Motive' in this play: 'durch die langen Parodie-Partien erhält das Befreiungsmotiv starke Selbständigkeit, während das Motiv des Gerichts über Euripides derart zurücktritt, daß V.1160ff. der Streit sehr rasch beigelegt wird, um die Befreiung zum Ende zu führen; dabei könnte sich die Befreiung nach der Versöhnung eigentlich sogar erübrigen. Die komischen Intentionen dominieren über die dramatische Ökonomie.'[104] Like similar analyses of *Frogs*, this scarcely does justice to the causal interrelation of the 'motifs': the rescue becomes important because of the miscarriage of a plan to influence the women's decision. Although the resolution of the dispute between the women and Euripides is somewhat perfunctory, its mechanism is causally adequate: Euripides in effect surrenders and gives the women a pledge of his future good behaviour. The very fact that Aristophanes does take the trouble to untie both nodes of his plot – that the initial problem is not simply superseded and left unresolved – is significant of his care over plot-structure.[105] Dramatic economy is not neglected, therefore, although it is (of course) true that comic intentions are dominant, in the sense that just how and when the plot is resolved is determined by the comic effects at which Aristophanes is aiming.

Dramatic economy is not neglected, but is dominated by comic intention. A well-constructed plot, that is to say, is *a* goal of Aristophanic comedy, but not *the* goal – for it is in turn functionally subordinate to the play's comic effects. One could therefore look on plot as an indispensable unifying element in Aristophanes; it affords the organised and organising framework within which those comic effects may be developed. Our earlier denials that Aristophanes was particularly

---

[103] Another bridge across the parabasis is the fetching of the Prytanis: set in motion in 762–4, and taken up in 922–9; this entry is carefully placed to foil the *Helen*-rescue, and – by changing the relative's mode of confinement – to motivate the choice of *Andromeda* for the next rescue attempt.

[104] P. Rau, 'Das Tragödienspiel in den "Thesmophoriazusen"', in: *Aristophanes und die alte Komödie*, ed. H.-J. Newiger (*Wege der Forschung* 265, Darmstadt 1975) 347.

[105] Cratinus, we learn from Platonius, began his plots well, but failed to follow them through to the end (εὔστοχος δὲ ὢν ἐν ταῖς ἐπιβολαῖς τῶν δραμάτων καὶ διασκευαῖς εἶτα προϊὼν καὶ διασπῶν τὰς ὑποθέσεις οὐκ ἀκολούθως πληροῖ τὰ δράματα: II 6–8 Koster) – a point to which we shall return. (Platonius' source is likely to have been the 3rd century Alexandrian critic Dionysiades of Mallos; see R. Pfeiffer, *History of Classical Scholarship* [Oxford 1968] 160.)

concerned with the thematic integration of his plays would imply that, within the causal frame established by the plot, the comic effects will be pursued centrifugally. This, too, can be observed in *Thesmophoriazusae*. The play consists largely of a series of Euripidean burlesques, but Euripides is hardly a consistent *target* of those burlesques, since in each case the humour derives mainly from the intrusion of some grotesque and alien element into a promising tragic idea: the climax of the *Telephus*-burlesque is a refurbishing of the stock joke against bibulous women; the *Helen* is rendered comic (apart from the general incongruity of the situation) by the interjections of the old woman, *Andromeda* by the mischievous Echo[106] and by the interjections of the Scythian. The diversity of targets and of sources of humour drawn together in this play is striking; there is no need to find an integrating theme – nor, indeed, has this been done with any plausibility.[107]

To discuss unity in terms of plot is inevitably to recall Aristotle; is it conceivable, then, that Aristophanic comedy is unified in an Aristotelian sense? The answer to that question will depend, obviously, on one's interpretation of Aristotle's theory of unity, as well as on one's reading of Aristophanes, and it is not possible to discuss the *Poetics* in detail here.[108] Some brief observations can be made, however. First,

---

[106] How can the idea that Echo is Euripides disguised have survived (e.g., H. Hansen, *Philologus* 120 [1976] 181–3)? She is evidently on stage at 1090–6, when the Scythian chases her, but Euripides has to be ready for his entry as Perseus at 1098 (presumably she enters at 1056 and retires to an inconspicuous corner at 1064: see Fraenkel [n.96] 22–6, O. Taplin, *The Stagecraft of Aeschylus* [Oxford 1977] 334–5). The joke in 1059–61 depends on a literalisation, which is spoilt if Echo is not Echo but Euripides. When Euripides does appear in disguise, he never sustains the role so consistently. And why on earth should Euripides do such a thing? His role is that of rescuer.

[107] For example, Hansen (n.106) 184: 'one should ask whether the play ultimately has two subjects or one: can the supposed failure of Agathon and Euripides as tragic poets, and the various perversions of sexual roles, be seen as aspects of the same phenomenon? ... The play ... is really a study of infertility or sterility, poetic as well as sexual, of barren wombs and barren minds, of the failure both to create and to procreate.' But where is it suggested that Euripides is 'barren'? The emphasis is rather on the fertility of his invention (93–4, 926–7); his failure is due to the stupidity of his audience (1128–32). 'Agathon's sexuality is linked closely with the quality of his literary output...; Euripides plays a woman not once but twice' (p. 184): not twice (he does not play Echo – see previous note) but once – and that is *after* he has given up his customary tragic mode for a cruder, more comic device (1160–1209).

[108] I have summarised my view of Aristotle's theory in the relevant section of my own *Poetics* (n.89), and will discuss the point in greater detail elsewhere.

Aristotle's criterion of unity is not addressed directly to the dramatic (or epic) text as such, but rests solely on the analysis of plot – a play is unified if its plot is unified; that is to say, Aristotle is working at a certain level of abstraction from the text. Secondly, what he requires of a plot is modest: its elements must follow one from another 'in accordance with necessity or probability' – that is, in due causal sequence; and the series of sequential events must be complete – it must have a beginning and end as defined in *Poet.* 1450b26–30.[109] It will be evident at once that Aristotle's approach does not require, indeed displays no interest in, the thematic integration of dramatic texts; it is only causal integration that is required – the view taken here of Aristophanes. Secondly, Aristotle's theory admits the extension of a plot beyond the resolution of a play's initial problematic if (as evidently may be the case) that extension is causally consequential. Most important, however, is an implication of Aristotle's abstraction from text to plot. Commentators have not sufficiently observed the difference between saying (i) that a play must dramatise a unified (that is, a continuous and complete) plot, and saying (ii) that a play must contain *only* the dramatisation of such a plot. Aristotle is committed to (i), but not to (ii); and this is important, because (i), unlike (ii), permits the text of a play to contain elements which digress from the underlying plot. On this view, while the causal integration of the *plot* must be strict, the causal integration of the *play* may be handled liberally (with thematic integration still not a requirement). This is precisely the practice of Aristophanes, for although the plays we have examined are based on carefully organised plots, they also contain much which, while still contributing to the overall effect of the play, does not contribute to the development of the plot: isolated jokes and comic routines, digressive lyrics, and – above all – the parabasis.

Richard Janko has recently argued in an impressive study of Aristotle's theory of comedy that the *Tractatus Coislinianus* derives from an epitome of the lost second book of Aristotle's *Poetics*; he also argues that Aristotle regarded Aristophanes as a comic ideal – as 'middle' comedy, in the sense which that term originally bore when Middle Comedy was new and New Comedy yet to develop. These 'astounding heterodoxies', as Janko calls them, seem to me probably cor-

---

[109] That Aristotle would have applied these criteria flexibly is suggested by his tolerance of concealed 'irrationalities' in plots (60a11–60b2), and by his recognition that 'impossibilities' can be justified if they enhance the poetic effect (60b22–9).

rect.[110] Even without venturing onto this controversial ground, however, a convergence of Aristophanic practice and Aristotelian principle is more probable than is widely supposed. Aristotle, after all, reached his theoretical conclusions by reflecting on the practice of the best poets; and even within the extant *Poetics* there is evidence that he thought Aristophanes to comedy what Sophocles was to tragedy and Homer to epic (the choice of these three paradigms in 48a25–8 can hardly be insignificant). Moreover, Aristotle himself dates the introduction of comedy structured by plot into Athens before Aristophanes; it was Crates, he says, who first abandoned the iambic form and composed 'universalised' (that is, necessary or probable) plots (49b5–9, cf. ch.9).[111] Later evidence concurs with this dating. Of the treatises on comedy edited by Koster, one describes Pherecrates as a follower of Crates in this development (III 29–31).[112] Another sees Cratinus as moving away from the disorder (ἀταξία) of 'old' comedy, but failing to complete the move; this was left to Aristophanes, who indeed at the end of his career developed 'new' (i.e., Middle) comedy (V 15–27). We have already mentioned (n.105) Platonius' observation that Cratinus began his plots well, but failed to follow them to the end (II 6–8). This consensus strongly supports the view that plot-structure is fundamental to Aristophanic comedy.

I have argued, therefore, that unity in Aristophanic comedy is unity of plot, liberally conceived so as to permit digression in the text that realises the plot; 'digression' must be understood here as *causal* rather than as *thematic* digression, for the simple reason that the thematic integration typically sought by recent criticism is not one of Aristophanes' goals. I have also suggested that this account of Aristophanic

---

[110] R. Janko, *Aristotle on Comedy* (London 1984) 87. I venture a few adverse comments: (i) on p. 244 Janko misinterprets *EN* 1128a31 (σκώπτειν is parallel to λοιδορεῖν, and one must supply κωλύειν): this weakens his case; (ii) his reference on p. 236 to Aristotle's views on unity and digression seems to me superficial and mistaken: my own account makes Aristotelian approval of Aristophanic comedy considerably more plausible; (iii) 'Plot is not as fully paramount as in *Poet.*, because the Treatise is not dealing with Menander' (p. 216): this is dangerous – plot is essential to Aristophanes also; the crucial point is that Aristotle has already discussed plot at length in the first book, and can take that discussion for granted in the second book.

[111] 'Abandoning the iambic ἰδέα' does not mean abandoning abuse, but abandoning the non-mimetic form of iambic abuse, that is, inserting abuse into the framework of a continuous and complete plot. Schwinge (n.92) 183–5 completely misunderstands this point.

[112] If Koster correctly defends αὖ as 'in vicem: ut iam Crates'; in context, after the mention of Pherecrates' rivalry with Crates, this seems likely.

unity is Aristotelian; this conclusion should not be thought strange, since Aristotle himself and other Greek critics can be shown to have dated the origins of plot-structured comedy in Athens to the middle of the fifth century, considerably before the beginning of Aristophanes' career. If this is correct, Aristophanes and his co-practitioners of the comic art in the 420s inherited a comic form based on carefully structured plots, and developed that form further; it follows that Aristophanes' latest work does not, as is often thought, represent a new and surprising departure, but continues to develop a trend that antedates his earliest extant work. But this is not the place to pursue further the literary-historical implications of these conclusions.

# Bibliography

J. T. Allen, 'On Suidas' biography of Aristophanes and the date of the second performance of the *Frogs*', *UCPCP* 11 (1930/3) 143–61.

D. Bain, 'A misunderstood scene in Sophokles, *Oidipous*', *G&R* 26 (1979) 132–45.

D. Barrett (tr.), *Aristophanes: The Wasps, The Poet and the Women, The Frogs* (Harmondsworth 1964).

J. du Boulay, *Portrait of a Greek Mountain Village* (Oxford 1974).

A. M. Bowie, 'The parabasis in Aristophanes: prolegomena, *Acharnians*', *CQ* 32 (1982) 27–40.

G. A. H. Chapman, 'Aristophanes and history', *Acta Classica* 21 (1978) 59–70.

G. Daux, 'Sur quelques passages du "Banquet" de Platon', *REG* 55 (1942) 237–58.

J. K. Davies, *Wealth and the Power of Wealth in Classical Athens* (New York 1981).

R. Dawe (ed.), *Sophocles: Oedipus Rex* (Cambridge 1982).

J. D. Denniston, *The Greek Particles*[2] (Oxford 1954).

K. J. Dover, 'Aristophanes' speech in Plato's *Symposium*', *JHS* 86 (1966) 41–50.

– (ed.), *Aristophanes: Clouds* (Oxford 1968).

–, *Aristophanic Comedy* (London 1972).

–, *Greek Popular Morality* (Oxford 1974).

–, *Greek Homosexuality* (London 1978).

M. I. Finley, *The Use and Abuse of History* (London 1975).

C. W. Fornara, 'Evidence for the date of Herodotus' publication', *JHS* 91 (1971) 25–34.

W. G. Forrest, 'Aristophanes' *Acharnians*', *Phoenix* 17 (1963) 1–12.

E. Fraenkel, *Beobachtungen zu Aristophanes* (Rome 1962).

T. Gelzer, 'Aristophanes', *RE Suppl.* XII (1970) 1392–1569.

A. W. Gomme, 'Aristophanes and politics', *CR* 52 (1938) 97–109.

–, 'Four passages in Thucydides', *JHS* 71 (1951) 70–80.

–, 'The interpretation of καλοὶ κἀγαθοί in Thucydides 4.40.2', *CQ* 3 (1953) 65–8.

–, *More Essays in Greek History and Literature* (Oxford 1962).

S. Halliwell, 'Aristophanes' apprenticeship', *CQ* 30 (1980) 33–45.

–, 'Ancient interpretations of ὀνομαστὶ κωμῳδεῖν in Aristophanes', *CQ* 34 (1984) 83–8.

–, 'Aristophanic satire', *Yearbook of English Studies* 14 (1984) 6–20.

H. Hansen, 'Aristophanes' *Thesmophoriazusae*: Theme, Structure, Production', *Philologus* 120 (1976) 165–85.

M. H. Hansen, 'How many Athenians attended the *Ecclesia*?', *GRBS* 17 (1976) 115–34.

–, 'The duration of a meeting of the Athenian *Ecclesia*', *CP* 74 (1979) 43–9.

–, *The Athenian Ecclesia* (Copenhagen 1983).

M. F. Heath, *The Poetics of Greek Tragedy* (London, 1987).

J. Henderson, 'Lysistrate: the play and its themes', *YCS* 26 (1980) 153–218.

A. O. Hulton, 'The women on the Acropolis', *G&R* 19 (1972) 32–9.

R. Janko, *Aristotle on Comedy* (London 1984).

R. Kassel – C. Austin, *Poetae Comici Graeci* (Berlin/New York 1983–).

K. D. Koch, *Kritische Idee und komisches Thema* (Bremen 1965).

T. Kock, *Comicorum Atticorum Fragmenta* (Leipzig 1880–88).

W. J. W. Koster, *Prolegomena de Comoedia* (*Scholia in Aristophanem* IIA, Groningen 1975).

W. Labov, *Language in the Inner City* (Oxford 1977).

M. Landfester, *Handlungsverlauf und Komik in den frühen Komödien des Aristophanes* (Berlin/New York 1977).

D. M. Lewis, 'Who was Lysistrata?', *BSA* 50 (1955) 1–12.

D. M. MacDowell (ed.), *Aristophanes: Wasps* (Oxford 1971).

–, 'Aristophanes and Kallistratos', *CQ* 32 (1982) 21–6.

–, 'The nature of Aristophanes' *Akhnarnians*', *G&R* 30(1983)143–62.

K. McLeish, *The Theatre of Aristophanes* (London 1980).

A. Meineke, *Fragmenta Comicorum Graecorum* (Berlin 1839–57).

C. Moulton, *Aristophanic Poetry* (Hypomnemata 68, Göttingen 1981).

H.-J. Newiger, 'War and peace in the comedy of Aristophanes', *YCS* 26 (1980) 219–37 (= 'Krieg und Frieden in der Komödie des Aristophanes', in: ΔΩPHMA: *Hans Diller zum 70. Geburtstag* [Athens 1975] 175–94).

A. W. Pickard-Cambridge, *The Dramatic Festivals of Athens*[2] (Oxford 1968).

R. Pfeiffer, *History of Classical Scholarship* (Oxford 1968).

K. Plepelits, *Die Fragmente der Demen des Eupolis* (Vienna 1970).

P. Rau, 'Das Tragödienspiel in den "Thesmophoriazusen"', in: *Aristophanes und die alte Komödie*, ed. H.-J. Newiger (*Wege der Forschung* 265, Darmstadt 1975) 339–56.

P. J. Rhodes, *The Athenian Boule* (Oxford 1972).

–, *A Commentary on the Aristotelian Athenaion Politeia* (Oxford 1981).

E. Ruschenbusch, 'Die Einführung des Theorikon', *ZPE* 36 (1979) 303–8.

G. E. M. de Ste Croix, *The Origins of the Peloponnesian War* (London 1972).

–, *The Class Struggle in the Ancient Greek World* (London 1981).

E. R. Schwinge, 'Zur Ästhetik der Aristophanischen Komödie am Beispiel der Ritter', *Maia* 27 (1975) 177–99.

C. P. Segal, 'The character and cults of Dionysus and the unity of the *Frogs*', *HSCP* 65 (1961) 207–42.

G. M. Sifakis, *Parabasis and Animal Choruses* (London 1971).

A. H. Sommerstein, 'Aristophanes, *Frogs* 1463–5', *CQ* 24 (1974) 24–7.

– (ed.), *Aristophanes: Acharnians* (Warminster 1980).

– (ed.), *Aristophanes: Knights* (Warminster 1981).

– (ed.), *Aristophanes: Wasps* (Warminster 1983).

–, 'Aristophanes and the demon poverty', *CQ* 34 (1984) 314–33.

O. Taplin, *The Stagecraft of Aeschylus* (Oxford 1977).

H. Tredennick (tr.), *Plato: The Last Days of Socrates* (Harmondsworth 1954).

R. G. Ussher (ed.), *Aristophanes: Ecclesiazusae* (Oxford 1973).

J. Vaio, '*Wasps*: the final scenes', *GRBS* 12 (1971) 335–51.

–, 'The manipulation of theme and plot in Aristophanes' *Lysistrata*', *GRBS* 14 (1973) 369–80.

M. L. West, *Studies in Greek Elegy and Iambus* (Berlin/New York 1974).

H. D. Westlake, 'The *Lysistrata* and the war', *Phoenix* 34 (1980) 38–54).

N. G. Wilson, 'Observations on Aristophanes' *Lysistrata*', *GRBS* 23 (1982) 157–63.

# Index of Ancient Authors

Aeschines 25
Aeschylus
  *Oresteia* 42
Andocides
  1.73–80: 20, 28
Archilochus
  fr. 5 W: 28
Archippus
  fr. 45 K: 34
Aristotle
  *EN* 1128a6–8: 26–7
    1128a30–1: 27, 53
  *Poet.* 51–3
  *Pol.* 1336b3–23: 27
  *Rhet.* 1417b4–5: 25
Aristophanes
  *Acharnians* 14, 16–19, 21, 22–3, 27,
    37, 40, 41
    377–82: 16, 17
    440–7: 16, 17
    496–556: 16, 17, 22
    595–619: 29–30, 31, 33, 40
    626–664: 18, 19, 21, 23, 43
    676–718: 19, 22, 33, 34, 40
    729–835: 35
  *Babylonians* 16
  *Banqueters* 34
  *Birds*
    186: 35
    268–90: 28
    445–6: 13
    640: 35
    723–36: 19
    752–68: 19, 21
    785–800: 19
    1337–71: 21
    1470–81: 28
  *Clouds* 9–12, 21, 24, 33, 41
    101: 29
    319–21: 11
    353–4: 28
    518–27: 13, 23

    537–44: 19
    549: 42
    576: 22
    607–26: 22
    943: 17
    1096–1104: 22
    1201–3: 22
  *Ecclesiazusae* 23–4
    197–8: 31
    205–8: 31
    214–28: 23–4
    433–40: 22
    677–80: 21, 24–5
  *Frogs* 19–21, 23, 24, 44–8
    274–6: 22
    367–8: 26–7
    686–705: 19–20, 43
    718–37: 20, 36
    739–40: 34
    907–79: 20
    916–7: 45
    1008–85: 20
    1036–8: 28
    1065–9: 29
    1411–81: 20, 21, 34, 45–6, 48
  *Knights* 7, 12–13, 22, 23–4, 31, 36, 40,
    41
    178–9: 37
    223–4: 31
    225–8: 30
    264–5: 31
    565–80: 40
    738–40: 29, 36
    749–55: 22
    801–9: 40
    1111–50: 21, 31
    1207–28: 40
    1274–5: 28, 29
    1323: 24
    1335–57: 21, 31
    1372: 29
    1373–81: 33

*Nic.* 8: 35
  *Mor.* 10cd: 26
Sannyrio
  fr. 9: 26
Sophocles 53
  *OT* 46
Telecleides
  fr. 39: 11
  fr. 40: 11
  fr. 41: 35

Theognis
  453–6: 25
Thucydides 35
Xenophon
  *Symp.* 6.8–10: 26
[Xenophon]
  2.18: 13, 42
  1.6, 9: 30

# General Index

Aeschylus 20–1, 24, 45, 47
Agathon 10, 11, 49
Alcibiades 10, 20, 34
assembly 12, 13, 22
audience 8, 12, 13, 18, 22–4, 26, 37, 38–41
Callistratus 16
Cimon 24, 34
Cleisthenes 49
Cleon 12, 13, 16–18, 25, 26, 27, 30, 35–7, 40
Cleonymus 28
*demos* 12, 13, 21–4, 31, 32, 36, 37, 38–41, 42, 43
dramatic illusion 16, 22
ἐπιχαιρεκακία 35
Euripides 11, 16–17, 20–1, 24, 33, 45–7, 49

fantasy 8, 14, 15, 23, 24, 37, 41–2
καλὸς κἀγαθός 29–31, 41
χρηστός 29–31, 33, 34, 40, 41
Laches 32
legal restraints 27
Lysimache 15
μισθοφορία 31, 39–40
Nicias 35
oratory 15, 25, 37, 38
Pantacles 28
parabasis 18–23, 40, 43, 47–9, 52
Patrocleides 21
Pericles 12, 23
Socrates 9–11, 12, 26, 29
Sophocles 45, 47
'sounds' 25–6
theoric fund 13

# Index of Modern Scholars

# Tragicorum Graecorum Fragmenta (TrGF)

## Vol. 1: Didascaliae Tragicae, Catalogi Tragicorum et Tragoediarum. Testimonia et Fragmenta Tragicorum Minorum

Editor: Bruno Snell. Editio correctior et addendis aucta. Curavit Richard Kannicht. 2., verbesserte und ergänzte Auflage der Ausgabe von 1971. 1986. XII, 363 Seiten, Leinen

„Ein Arbeitsmittel … bei dem sich eminente Sorgfalt und Gelehrsamkeit mit der größten Übersichtlichkeit präsentieren." *Anzeiger für die Altertumswissenschaft*

## Vol. 2: Fragmenta Adespota

Testimonia Volumini 1 Addenda. Indices ad Volumina 1 et 2. Editor: Richard Kannicht und Bruno Snell. 1981. XIX, 453 Seiten, Leinen

„Il est rare d'avoir sous les yeux un ouvrage d'une perfection telle que toute critique semble mesquine et ingrate devant le travail accompli. C'est le cas pour ce deuxième volume des *Tragicorum Graecorum Fragmenta* …
Ce volume réunit non seulement les *adespota* connus par des citations (= Nauck), mais aussi tous les fragments tragiques retrouvés sur papyrus, non identifiés … Des introductions brèves mais substantielles, pleines d'érudition, précèdent chaque fragment et l'apparat critique est d'une précision exemplaire." *Antiquité Classique*

## Vol. 3: Aeschylus

Editor: Stefan Radt. 1985. 592 Seiten, Leinen

Dieser Band enthält außer sämtlichen zitierten und auf Papyrus wiedergefundenen Resten der verlorenen Dramen des Aischylos auch die Zeugnisse über Aischylos' Leben und Werk sowie ein Verzeichnis seiner teils sicher bezeugten teils von den Modernen erschlossenen Tri- und Tetralogien; außerdem ein Supplement zu Italies *Index Aeschyleus*, ein Quellenverzeichnis und Zahlenkonkordanzen zu den Ausgaben von Mette, sowie ausführliche Ergänzungen und Berichtigungen zu den Sophoklesfragmenten in Band 4.

## Vol. 4: Sophocles

Editor: Stefan Radt. 1977. 731 Seiten, Leinen

„Was den Apparat der von Radt besorgten Edition anbelangt, so sind hier mit einer bewunderungswerten Ausführlichkeit und Genauigkeit alle Quellen und Zeugnisse für jedes Fragment angegeben und mit höchster Akribie alle Lesarten und Vorschläge zur Textgestaltung verzeichnet. Das bezieht sich in gleichem Maße sowohl auf die Fragmente selbst als auch auf die ihnen beigefügten Zeugnisse.
Die Ausgabe der Sophokleischen Fragmente von Radt … zieht die Bilanz des bisher Erreichten und bereitet einen zuverlässigen Boden für neue Forschungen für mehrere Jahrzehnte." *Deutsche Literaturzeitung*

Der Band 5 **Euripides** (Editor: Richard Kannicht) wird vorbereitet.

Bitte fordern Sie den Sonderprospekt *Tragicorum Graecorum Fragmenta (TrGF)* an.

V&R Vandenhoeck & Ruprecht · Göttingen

# Josef-Hans Kühn / Ulrich Fleischer
# INDEX HIPPOCRATICUS

Cui elaborando interfuerunt sodales Thesauri Linguae Graecae Hamburgensis. Curas postremas adhibuerunt K. Alpers, A. Anastassiou, D. Irmer, V. Schmidt.

---

Das Werk erscheint in 4 Lieferungen im Umfang von je etwa 230 bis 280 Seiten (zweispaltig, im Lexikonformat).

**Fasc.I: A–Δ**. 1986. XXXIV, 200 Seiten, broschiert

**Fasc.II: E–K**. 1987. 264 Seiten, broschiert

Die Lieferungen 3 und 4 werden 1988/89 erscheinen.

---

In diesem Index wird der vollständige Wortschatz sämtlicher Schriften des Corpus Hippocraticum dokumentiert (ausgenommen sind nur der Artikel und einige Partikeln). Zitiert wird nach der bis heute wichtigsten, wiederholt nachgedruckten Gesamtausgabe von E. Littré. Diese Grundlage wird erweitert um einige nicht bei Littré gedruckte Texte und die Lemmata der Glossare Erotians und Galens, soweit sie in den erhaltenen hippokratischen Schriften nicht nachweisbar sind; vor allem aber ergänzt und korrigiert durch systematische Auswertung der neueren kritischen Ausgaben und des handschriftlichen Befundes. Das eingeschlagene Verfahren verbindet zwei Vorteile: einheitliche Zitierweise nach Littré und reichhaltige Angaben zur Überlieferung aller, insbesondere der noch nicht kritisch neuedierten Schriften. – In der Darbietung hält der Index die Mitte zwischen bloßem Stellenverzeichnis und Lexikon. Gegliedert wird primär nach grammatischen Kategorien und Bedeutungsunterschieden; ferner werden besondere Wortverbindungen und bemerkenswerte Dialektformen herausgehoben. Auch ist weniger gewöhnlichen Wörtern eine Übersetzung (in Latein) beigegeben. – Vorausgeschickt ist (in deutscher Sprache) eine sachliche Einleitung, die u.a. ein Verzeichnis der hippokratischen Schriften mit Angaben zur Überlieferung, zu den Ausgaben und wenn möglich zur Datierung enthält.

Bitte fordern Sie den Sonderprospekt *Index Hippocraticus* an.

---

V&R Vandenhoeck & Ruprecht · Göttingen